THE HEALTHY GOURMET COOKBOOK

BARBARA BASSETT

Also by Barbara Bassett

The Healthy Gourmet International Cookbook

THE HEALTHY GOURMET COOKBOOK

BARBARA BASSETT

HOW TO USE NATURAL FOOD DELICIOUSLY

Arlington Books
King Street St. James's
London

THE HEALTHY GOURMET COOKBOOK
First published 1985 by
Arlington Books (Publishers) Ltd
London S.W.1

© *1985 Barbara Bassett*

Typeset by Inforum Ltd, Portsmouth
Printed and bound by
The Guernsey Press, Guernsey

British Library Cataloguing in Publication Data
Bassett, Barbara
The healthy gourmet cookbook.
1. Cookery
641.5   TX717

ISBN 0–85140–662–9

Contents

Introduction

The dictionary defines gourmet as "a connoisseur in eating and drinking." We found that a connoisseur is "one aesthetically versed in any subject . . . competent to act as a critical judge of an art, or in a matter of taste." Not just someone with a penchant for rich sauces or a flair for whipping up a beef Wellington, a gourmet is one who appreciates and discerns that which is beautiful in eating and drinking.

We are all aware that tastes are made, not born, and we are learning just how much manipulation of taste exists, especially in food processing, advertising and sales. Man is a relentless pursuer of the beautiful but he is also an incessant manipulator. We turn unspoiled woodlands into sterile housing projects or unimaginative parks, literally missing the forest for the trees. Our overwhelming curiosity leads us to take things apart and try something new. It may be true that you never know 'til you try, and you may just make a wonderful discovery. If your something new turns out wrong, you don't have to stick with it. But if you are a large corporation with millions of dollars invested in this not-so-hot whatsit, you will find a way to *sell* it, not scrap it. Invest a few hundred thousand more pounds to make your whatsit look attractive. Convince as many people as possible that owning a whatsit will make them instant social successes, discerning consumers, and attractive to the opposite sex! A TV commercial comes to mind in which a sexy-looking lady opens a tin of tomato-flour-meat-spice mixture, pours it over a white hamburger bun, and her man comes racing into the kitchen! This one is funny, but the ads aimed at your children aren't!

The implication to a child that Sugar-Goos can make

him popular, attractive and happy can make it exceedingly difficult for him to refuse the stuff and risk being sad, puny and friendless! Luckily, even very small children recognize the truth, that Mummy will be very happy if he *doesn't* buy Sugar-Goos, and furthermore that any kid who eats Sugar-Goos will be a fat, listless kid with cavities.

What this has to do with beauty is simply that truth is beautiful to everyone, except to those with an investment in falsehood. For instance, the FDA list of "action levels for natural or unavoidable defects in food for human use." This list tells how much spoilage or filth is *allowed* in your food *before* the *FDA* will take any action. Publishing the list may seem like an honest gesture, except that the food manufacturers do *not* publish how many insect particles or rodent hairs are actually *in* your peanut butter. They know you wouldn't buy their un-beautiful peanut butter unless you could just ignore those hundred or so insect fragments per cup. You would wait for, search for, or make your own honest, beautiful, pure, clean peanut butter — a peanut butter fit for a gourmet!

A major food processor once defended the excessive saltiness of his food by explaining that salt is the *lowest* common denominator of human taste. Obviously, he was not seeking the gourmet trade! Not that being a gourmet makes one an automatic snob. On the contrary; simple, ungarnished, unadorned food is often the best. Homely, coarse brown bread; creamy farmhouse cheeses; ripe, red tomatoes just off the vine; brown rice with the bran intact, porridge of rough crushed oats with dark amber honey — these are the simple things of earth and the good things.

New Foods

What we make of these good things is also very much a matter of taste. In cooking, we have to contend with individual tastes and prejudices as well as those that are regional and national. James Beard had a cooking show on a Canadian T.V. network on which he prepared a few dishes while several ladies watched and then sampled the food. One might assume that the comments and questions might mirror those of the home viewer. However, one day Mr. Beard prepared what appeared to be a delicious chicken liver rissoto — and not one of those women had ever tasted a chicken liver before!

Raw fish is a Japanese delicacy. The French have a passion for snails, as do the Italians, who also do marvellous things with squid. Species of caterpillar are eaten in Africa, though they are said to be rather bland. What of tripe, chitterlings, brains in black butter and caper sauce? What daring souls first tasted the shoots of asparagus and bamboo, pried open the stubborn oyster, dug peanuts from the ground, ate the stems of rhubarb whose leaves are deadly poison?

We have all tried new foods and found them not to our taste, and we have found new tastes that delight us. The more new things we try and classify, the more we are competent to judge those foods. Cooking is indeed an art, although its frustrating built-in annihilation factor drives some cooks to perfection and others out of the kitchen forever. Luckily, failures are as short-lived as triumphs and need not be repeated.

Improvisation

Cooking is an improvisational art and all great cooks know it, perhaps instinctively. No really good cook panics for the lack of some ingredient. Making the best of what is available is the basis of all regional cuisines and the secret of every exciting new dish. Take the time and trouble to learn which foods are native to your area, and which are produced or grown in your region. Find out what ripens when. You don't need to live on a farm to take advantage of all the information available. To get the best, go as close to the source as possible. Grow your own, find a friendly farmer, look for a farm shop or retail outlet that carries produce grown locally on organic farms. Try things from health-food stores that you usually buy at the supermarket. Mayonnaise, for instance, is great without stabilizers, thickeners, etc.

Good food . . . really good food . . . is healthy food,

nourishing to the body, a delight to the senses, a pleasure to the soul. You can't say that about tinned spaghetti — ads notwithstanding. But then, it's a matter of taste.

The very best cooks in the world, from Chinese peasant to French master chef, have more in common than just a love of good food. They have an appreciation and respect for the quality of the ingredients they use. The finest dish can't be any better than the ingredients that make it up. What does this mean to those of us who are interested in healthful food? Everything. If you are interested enough to search out the foods which are freshest, ripest and most nutritious, you will find yourself with the tastiest foods. For instance, white flour has less flavour than whole wheat and freshly ground flour is, of course, superior to stale. Frozen vegetables have more flavour than tinned; ripe, fresh vegetables are better than frozen and anyone who has ever eaten just-picked organically grown vegetables know that those are the best-tasting of all!

Technology

There are people who advocate a wholesale dismissal of modern technology, a return to simpler, more primitive existence. It is true that some small groups, such as the Hunzas, have achieved healthy, happy lives far away from our mechanized society. Nevertheless, few of us would wish to toss aside all the benefits of our modern world, and even if we did — how many could the mountaintops of Hunzaland support? If we use what we have intelligently, we have the resources to become the best nourished society on earth. We have shipping that brings to our doorstep foods which would otherwise be unavailable.

Not long ago, oranges were a rare and expensive treat. Certainly, local produce in season is the freshest, but it's great to be able to get brown rice in Devon, whole wheat in Perthshire. We have resources for storing food. The vegetables we grow organically in the summer are frozen for the winter, rescuing us from dependence on "store bought" foods. Perhaps the greatest benefit of modern technology is the communications systems which disseminate information. New ideas don't reach us as months-old rumours. Instead, they are published, broadcast, discussed, analysed, disputed, supported, revised and enlarged upon.

We have more knowledge now about foods and nutrition than at any time in history. Our information may be confusing, or even misleading, but it *is there* for evaluation. We can make our own judgments based on knowledge rather than superstition. There are those who will not listen, always. There are those who do not care. But the number of people who are vitally concerned about the content and quality of the goods they eat is growing rapidly.

It's a revolutionary idea *not* to stuff your kids with candy but there *was* a time when sweets were few and far between. When they became so easily available, doting parents who had dreamed of sugar-plums at Christmas delighted in indulging their children with endless confections — and obesity and bad teeth. It was blissful ignorance and it resulted in flouridation programmes, amphetamine diet pills, and medical bills. We have seen the results. We are learning that preclusion is easier, cheaper and a lot more fun than the cure.

Health Foods

We still tend to think of "health foods" as grains, oils, dried fruits and vitamin preparations sold in special shops. Well, those *are* health foods. But in the not-so-remote past, everything we put on the table was fresh and free of the chemicals and pesticides which are now a part of our diet. When we moved away from the farms, we traded freshness and purity for convenience and availability. We cannot de-urbanize our world but we can revitalize our food.

We have learned to "fix up" the tasteless food we buy with sugar and salt. We must acquire new tastes, new ways of cooking and shopping for food. Whole grains won't sit on a shelf month after month, they need cold storage. Unsprayed fruits and vegetables may not be as pretty as pesticide-covered ones but they *do* taste better and they're safer! How would you feel if you were served tinned soup in a fine restaurant? If the restaurant is good, you get soup "from scratch," in other words — home cooking!

Cooking deliciously healthy food is easy — that's what this book is all about. *Buying* the best ingredients is not as simple. Luckily, health food outlets are springing up like mushrooms after a rainstorm. Some of them carry vegetables, dairy products and meats. The demand for meat and vegetables *without* pesticides, hormones, chemical fertilizers, preservatives, stabilizers, and artificial anything has far outstripped the supply. There are people unscrupulous enough to try to fill the gap with "organic" labels on products that are not at all organically raised or processed. Read labels warily. Check your sources as best you can.

There is a wide world of lovely food which will look very strange at first to the white-bread generation. *The Healthy Gourmet* will take the mystery and strangeness out of these foods and make them familiar and flavourful fare. Many of the things which might be new to us are the everyday staples of diet in other parts of the world. In fact, the most famous and elaborate dishes are simply imaginative combinations of homely things.

Cooking Creatively

A recipe should be a guide, not an adamant rule.

Cooking is a creative venture. It can be an endless kaleidoscope of flavour, colour and texture. The essence of pleasurable cooking is improvisation. Without it we are uncreative slaves of the printed recipe and tend to succumb to dull routine. Improvisation requires a knowledge of ingredients which allows the cook to predict with reasonable accuracy what will happen when a pinch of this is added to a handful of that.

Cooking for your best health involves using the best ingredients, getting the most nutritional mileage out of them and making the finished dish look and taste delectable. We have found recipes bursting with nourishing goodies, but drably tasteless or worse. Unless your family has *always* been on a super-healthful diet, you are going to find yourself introducing many new foods. You will need reliable recipes to get you started; recipes that are easy to prepare, versatile, and tasty enough to change "We never had *that* before!" to "When can we have this again?" You probably wouldn't buy tomatoes at all if you had only one recipe you used them in. Those one-dish ingredients always seem to get lost on the darkest shelf, and deservedly.

Economy

There are so many foods in the world, it would be impossible to taste them all in a lifetime. When you combine foods with each other — with herbs and spices — what an infinity of gustatory delights! There is a world of pleasure awaiting the inquisitive palate and the adventurous chef. Travelling is one way to sample these delights but the armchair (or kitchen chair) traveller can do as well — often better.

The great restaurants all over the world are often "haute cuisine" with a sprinkling of native places serving what they consider the finest indigenous dishes. What's missing is the homely peasant fare, which is often plain, healthful and delicious. Peasants are not usually as happy as kings. They must struggle to survive against heart-breaking odds. Without beginning a discussion of social inequality, it is obvious that poor folks, after all, usually have a pretty limited diet. The foods they live on *must* be cheap and nutritious. It is only in our plastic, modern supermarkets that cheap, convenient foods may have little or no nutritional value and the poor eat white bread, white sugar and potato chips! "Peasants" were once limited to coarse, brown bread, sweetened with honey, or spread with raw butter!

The most *inexpensive* foods are traditionally those which are fairly easy to grow, store and prepare. The Chinese, who do food things very well, *dry* such exotic perishables as oysters and lily buds and then use them later, sparingly, to flavour more homely fare.

What could be more homely than milk and wheat? A cow, a patch of grain — milk the cow, harvest the grain — nutritious and filling foods can be very soul-satisfying as well as supply the basic body needs. For nearly everyone, simple foods are the beloved fare of childhood and what may be exotic fare to one, will be "soul food" to another. Since no one, however sophisticated, really leaves behind the happy foods of childhood, and since, as we've said, these are often foods that store, and therefore transport well, foods from all over the world are available to us.

Using these foods to our best advantage involves not only being able to prepare them to make them palatable but adding a pinch of imagination and a dash of inspiration to make the ordinary *extraordinary*. Ingenious methods of preparing foods evolve from the desire to escape from the boredom of circumscribed fare. There must be very little waste of food when the pocketbook is slender. Consequently, there is often little waste of nutritional value. Cooking water, for instance, is too precious to throw down the drain with all its vitamins, minerals and flavour. Tough outer leaves, such as those from cabbage, are not discarded. In fact, if you take the cooking water, cabbage leaves and a few old crusts of brown bread, you have the basics for a peasant soup that my grandmother used to make.

One of the current economic facts of life is that food prices rise while our nutritional needs remain the same. The latest United States FDA recommended daily allowance calls for 45 to 65 grams of protein. That's about eight eggs or two quarts of milk or a pound of steak every day! Although protein needs may differ from one individual to another, enough minimum protein for a family of four can be a major expense. Since we can't cut down on protein, we must find ways to trim the cost.

Many excellent, and often overlooked, proteins occur in pulses, seeds, nuts and grains. Of the known amino acids, eight cannot be manufactured in the human body, and must be consumed every day. These eight are tryptophan, threonine, phenylalamine, lysine, valine, isoleucine, methionine-cystine and leucine. If a food is deficient in any one of the eight, the value of the remaining seven is lowered to that level of efficiency; therefore balancing the amino acids is essential.

Eggs, milk, meat, poultry and fish contain what is called "complete" protein. Other foods may contain excellent protein, too, but it must be balanced to make the protein completely available. It can't be done by eating a food high in some amino acids, and "catching up" later. The balancing amino acids must be ingested together. Soybeans, for instance, are limited in the amount of tryptophan and methionine-cystine they contain, but are particularly rich in lysine. Cereals and grains are low in lysine, but high in tryptophan and methionine-cystine. Eaten together, whether in one dish or simply at the same meal, they produce the complete protein needed to sustain life.

SOY FLOURS can be added to most baked goods as well as sauces, soups, etc. In fact, soy flour is routinely used by commercial bakers to produce goods that are moister and better-keeping. The lecithin that naturally occurs in soy flour also gives it a slightly emulsifying quality.

SOY GRANULES can be used in baking, too and in many other dishes. Their texture makes them a natural as an extender for ground meats. Soy flours contain from 11 to 14 grams of protein in $\frac{1}{4}$ cup, while granules contain about 19 grams in $\frac{1}{4}$ cup. These foods have the additional advantage of being naturally alkaline, thus balancing the acidity of grains and animal protein. Also, full-fat or "natural" soy flour, contains the natural oils of the soybean which are rich in lecithin as well as linoleic acid, known as an "*essential* fatty acid" because it cannot be synthesized in the body.

NUTRITIONAL YEAST (Brewers' or Torula) =

about 8 grams of protein per level tablespoon. Add it to vegetable juice drinks, soups, stews, sauces, gravies, sprinkle it on cereal. Shop around for a good-tasting yeast, there are several available.

WHEAT GERM = about 14 grams of protein per 2 oz.. Add it to baked goods, casseroles, sprinkle on cereals and salads, whiz it in a blender with fruit and vegetable juices.

LOW HEAT DRIED MILK = about 24 grams of protein per $\frac{1}{8}$ cup (dry). Dried milk is considerably cheaper than fresh milk, but contains the same amount and quality of protein if it is dried at low temperatures. Non-instant dry milk has undergone less processing than the instant type, it tastes better and is more versatile. It may be mixed with water and used as fresh milk, or added to fresh milk for a nutritional boost. The non-instant type may be added to baked goods, too.

BREAD — Whole wheat bread has about 20 percent more protein than white bread, and is even higher in protein when made with added soy flour.

NUTS AND SEEDS contain good but incomplete protein. Replace part of the amount in a recipe with soy granules to achieve a more balanced protein.

Individual Nutrition

Determining one's individual nutrient requirements is a complicated process which must take into account body size, age and physical activity. Recommended Daily Allowances are based on *average* needs, but nutritional needs vary from one individual to another. Also, individual needs may vary from day to day due to stress, illness, change of activity, etc.

The best "health insurance" is to *know* what you're eating. We once knew a lady who thought she and her son ate well, yet both had chronic intestinal pain. A diet analysis showed that their usual diet included very little Vitamin C and very few B vitamins. A change of diet brought relief to both, and a subsequent lapse brought a return of the symptoms! A farm family moving to a new area of the country were plagued by minor infections until they added supplementary zinc to their diets. They found that the soil in their new area was poor in zinc.

Unless you grow your own food, and know what nutrients are present, you'll often be buying devitalized food. Fresh produce loses nutrients during shipping and storage. Produce in your market may be trucked from distant farms whose soil is deficient in trace minerals. Shops like to display young, sweet carrots, although they contain less Vitamin A than older, tougher carrots.

There are some books which list the nutrients in foods, but not easily available and even with one of them at hand, much information will be lacking. For one thing, some foods are not listed. For another, not all *nutrients* are listed. Until more detailed analyses are available, we must rely on certain "super foods" known to contain various nutrients. These foods are used to boost the nutritional value of everyday meals.

Basically, we all need protein, fats and carbohydrate every day. We also need vitamins and minerals, some in minute amounts. Since nutrients act synergistically, *all* must be included in the daily diet.

Sources of Nutrients:

UNSATURATED FATTY ACIDS are found in liquid vegetable oils.

VITAMIN C; peppers, tomatoes, cherries, dark leaves.

VITAMIN A; liver, fish liver oils, egg yolks, milk, butter, dark leaves, apricots, yams, carrots, parsley.

VITAMIN D; fish liver oils, milk, bone meal.

VITAMIN E; seeds, grains, wheat germ oil, dark leaves, milk, eggs.

VITAMIN K; alfalfa, dark green leaves, liver.

BIOFLAVONOIDS; buckwheat, citrus pulp, red peppers, apricots.

VITAMIN B COMPLEX; liver, organ meats, grains, nuts, seeds, eggs, soy products, brewers' yeast.

B_{12}; meat, fish, poultry, dairy products, some brewers' yeast.

CHOLINE & INOSITOL; lecithin, soy products.

PABA; yogurt.

B_{15}; brewers' yeast, seeds, whole grains.

B_{17}; sprouts.

Minerals:

CALCIUM; dairy products, bone meal.

CHOLINE; kelp.

CHROMIUM; brewers' yeast, corn oil, liver, bone meal.

COBALT; meats.

COPPER; organ meats, shellfish, nuts, dried pulses.

FLUORIDE; tea, seafoods.

IODINE; seafoods, kelp, iodized salt.

IRON; liver, organ meats, dark green leaves, whole grains, dried fruits, molasses.

MAGNESIUM; milk, nuts, whole grains, dark green leaves, seafoods.

MANGANESE; nuts, seeds, grains, liver, dark green leaves, buckwheat, bone meal.

PHOSPHORUS; organ meats, fish, pulses, dairy products.

POTASSIUM; dark green leaves, wheat germ, sunflower seeds, citrus, pulses, fruits.

SELENIUM; brewers' yeast, garlic, liver, eggs.

ZINC; shellfish, protein foods, whole grains, brewers' yeast, pumpkin seeds.

SULPHUR; eggs, garlic, onions, meat, fish, pulses, seeds.

FIBRE; whole grains, seeds, nuts, vegetables, sprouts, pulses.

Multi-Nutrient Foods; liver, shell-fish, seafood, dairy products, dark green leaves (such as spinach), sweet red peppers, parsley, nuts, seeds, whole grains, fruits, eggs, soy products.

Super Foods:

ACEROLA CHERRIES; higher in Vitamin C than any other food.

ALFALFA; produces sprouts rich in Vitamins A and K.

BONE MEAL; source of calcium, chromium, manganese, Vitamin D.

BREWERS' YEAST; source of B vitamins, protein and trace minerals — some brands contain Vitamin B_{12}.

DESSICATED LIVER;* source of Vitamin A, B-complex, iron and trace minerals.

KELP; source of many trace minerals.

LECITHIN; contains choline and inositol.

ROSEHIPS; source of Vitamin C.

SPROUTS; source of vitamins and minerals.

WHEAT GERM; high in protein, B-complex, Vitamin E and minerals.

Protecting Your Nutrients:

1. Eat a great deal of raw foods, as heat destroys nutrients. Try one salad meal each day.

---

*NOTE: When using liver, always insist on organic or avoid it. Being the "filter" it is often loaded with toxic materials.

2. Store foods in dark places. B vitamins are especially vulnerable to light. Open shelf storage may be attractive but it's not particularly healthy.
3. Store foods in cool places and for very short times. Even under refrigeration, some nutrients are lost. In warm weather, get foods from shop cooler to *your* cooler as quickly as possible.
4. Include some poly-unsaturated fats with every meal. Vitamins A, D, E and K are fat-soluble.
5. Consuming all cooking, soaking and sprouting water conserves the water-soluble vitamins and minerals.
6. For table seasoning, use fresh lemon juice, kelp and vegetable salts, as they can add some vitamins and trace minerals.
7. Use parsley generously as an *edible* garnish — one tablespoonful contains nearly 3000 IU of Vitamin A!
8. Use herbs and spices to season foods while cooking. Table condiments such as ketchup contain sugar.
9. Avoid refined flours and sugar. They add nothing but calories to your diet, and may *increase* the need for certain nutrients.
10. Avoid nutrient-destructive items like coffee, alcohol, tobacco and food additives.

The most important fact to keep in mind is that *you* are not "average." Fulfilling the *minimum* daily requirements may not be enough for your personal needs. A small, sedentary person will probably need to pack a lot of nutrition into a small amount of food. Excess carbohydrate produces excess fat. Excess protein can be converted to carbohydrate, but the process causes some strain on the body. Saturated fats in meats and butter should be consumed in meagre amounts. Base your diet on multi-nutrient foods and use the super foods generously to bolster your nutrition.

Oils

More and more, health-conscious people are reading labels and questioning the additives in their food. Even seemingly innocuous foods, such as vegetable oils, can be found to contain a tongue-twisted galaxy of preservatives if one reads the (very) small print. These preservatives give the oils longer shelf life, both in the shop and in your home. That's what they do FOR you, but what they do TO you is another matter. BHA and BHT are two of the most common preservatives. In Ruth Winter's *A Consumer's Dictionary of Food Additives* (Crown, NY, 1972) it is reported that "pregnant mice fed a diet of one half of one per cent of BHT (or BHA . . .) gave birth to offspring that frequently had chemical changes in the brain and subsequent abnormal behaviour patterns."

Oils without preservatives can be found. It is best to refrigerate them after opening. Crude oils, dark in colour and rich in flavour, retain their natural anti-oxidants and are less subject to rancidity. They are best used in salads and marinades as they may darken and spatter in frying.

Liquid vegetable oils contain essential fatty acids which the body needs but cannot produce. These essential fatty acids are contained in polyunsaturated fats. Animal fats, including lard, butter and suet, are saturated fat and are fairly firm at room temperature. Un-saturated fats include both mono- and poly-unsaturates, and both are found in vegetable oils. The more poly-unsaturates an oil contains, the more clear and free-running it will be when refrigerated. Vegetable oils do not contain cholesterol.

There are three methods of extracting oils. The first uses a hydraulic press. By this method, olives and sesame seeds will produce oil when pressed cold — all other materials must be heated. The second method subjects cooked material to continuous pressure through a chamber with a rotating auger. This is called the "expeller" method. The third method is solvent extraction which mixes cooked material with a petroleum-based solvent. This solvent method is used by most commercial oil manufacturers and is the method which produces most of the oil found in supermarkets.

Oil which has been extracted but not refined is crude oil. Crude oil retains the natural flavour and aroma of the material from which it was extracted. It is dark in colour, and contains solid particles which may settle in the oil. It also contains Vitamin A, Vitamin E and phosphorous compounds such as lecithin.

Snacks & Appetizers

Snacking has become something of a national obsession. Partly, because we are still affluent enough to indulge in whimsical appetites, and partly because there is a fuzzy line between hunger and a desire to eat. Also, we are constantly bombarded with advertisements for the vast variety of foods that are meant to be eaten "between" meals. The sad truth is that overweight is nearly always the result of overconsumption, and a calorie is a calorie whether it is consumed before, during or after a proper meal. Sitting in front of the TV for a few hours isn't very conducive to calorie-burning, yet every few minutes there is a commercial for another "mouth-watering, taste-tempting treat." Look at all that food. Look at all the happy people eating. Doesn't it make you hungry? No. It only makes you want to eat.

Actually, there is nothing wrong with snacks *per se*. It is what they have become that is so disheartening. Of all the plastic, over-refined foods that glut the markets, "snacks" are probably the trashiest. One hundred grams of potato crisps, for instance, give you 533 calories, as much as 600 milligrams of sodium, and almost 40 grams of fat. A baked potato, on the other hand, has 76 calories in a hundred grams, $\frac{1}{10}$th of a gram of fat and 6 grams of sodium. In a hundred grams of cola drink (about $\frac{3}{4}$ of a glass) you get 39 calories, $10\frac{1}{2}$ grams of carbohydrates and virtually no nutrients at all. These figures are published in McCance & Widdowson's *The Composition of Foods*, as are similarly ugly truths about cakes and sweets.

Nutrition and snacking are not necessarily exclusive. In fact, there has been some research showing that frequent small meals may be more beneficial than the "three squares." A good-for-you snack preceding a lighter meal could be nutritionally beneficial. A trash-food snack followed by the same old heavy dinner is a primrose path to obesity and Heaven-knows-what else.

If three big meals a day is your idea of the good life, avoid snacks altogether. If you can get by with small meals and a few nourishing goodies in between, then you will enjoy a bit of nutritious snacking, and probably keep your figure as well. It's easy to keep a stock of *good* snack foods on hand. They can be enjoyed anytime — between meals, as *hors d'oeuvres*, after school, at midnight or even as light meals. The most basic supply of snacks, we think, would include the following:

Popcorn (remember popcorn?). Toss popped corn with a mixture of butter and cold-pressed oil, add a little vegetable salt.

Fruits of all kinds, both fresh and dried.

Nuts and seeds.

"Finger vegetables" such as carrots and celery.

Cheeses.

Yogurt.

Granola

Your imagination can supply a lot of other ideas. What you want to avoid are over-salted, over-sweetened foods that are nutritionally worthless.

The snack foods we have listed previously are mostly of the eat-and-run variety. Some of the recipes which follow can be put together in a matter of minutes, others require more preparation time, and you might wish to save them for *hors d'oeuvres*, but we sometimes like a bit of fancy snacking, so we have included them.

NOTE: If your children like junk snacks, start them into whole food snacking with the snack-kebabs. Try making smaller versions with toothpicks. Leave them in the refrigerator, and watch them disappear.

Snack Kebabs

Skewers   *Chunks of cheese*
Cherry tomatoes   *Chunks of celery*
Small spring onions   *Carrot slices*
Chunks of green pepper

Thread any or all of the above on the skewers. Eat as is, or serve with a yogurt dip.

VARIATION: Use fresh and dried fruits, separately, together and/or with chunks of cheese. Makes a nice dessert for picnics.

Stuffed Cherry Tomatoes

Cherry tomatoes   *Chives*
Cottage cheese

Cut the stem end from each tomato, and scoop out the inside. Fill the hollow with cottage cheese, and sprinkle with minced chives.

VARIATIONS: Mix the cottage cheese with cream cheese or blue cheese. Sprinkle with minced mint leaves or chopped nuts or seeds.

Sardine Bits

1 *tin sardines*   1 *teaspoon soy powder*
½ *small onion, minced*   ½ *teaspoon lemon juice*
½ *tsp. Dijon mustard*   4 *slices wholewheat toast*

Mash the sardines with the onion, mustard, soy powder and lemon juice. Spread on the toast. Cut the toast in quarters. Grill, sardine side up, for 3–5 minutes, or until lightly browned.

Makes 16 pieces.

Escargots Forestiere

2 *tablespoons butter*	1 *tablespoon minced parsley*
2 *tablespoons safflower oil*	12 *prepared snails*
1 *teaspoon minced chives*	12 *mushroom caps*
1 *clove garlic, crushed*	

Mix together the butter, oil, chives, garlic and parsley. Put a small amount of the mixture into each of the mushroom caps. Top with a snail. Add the remaining butter mixture on top of the snails. Grill, snail side up, for about 10 minutes, or until the butter is bubbly.
  Serves 2.

Marinated Mushrooms

½ *lb. fresh mushrooms*	2 *tablespoons minced parsley*
2 *tablespoons oil*	1 *clove garlic, crushed*
2 *tablespoons lemon juice*	1 *teaspoon dried thyme*
3 *tablespoons dry white wine*	½ *teaspoon pepper*
2 *tablespoons minced onion*	

Wipe mushrooms clean and cut a small slice from each stem and discard. Halve or quarter large mushrooms to make pieces of uniform size. Set mushrooms aside.
  Mix all remaining ingredients together in a saucepan. Bring to a boil and simmer 3 minutes. Add the mushrooms and stir to mix well. Cover the pan and simmer 3 minutes. Remove the cover and let simmer 3 minutes more, stirring occasionally. Let cool in marinade. Chill. Serve next day.
  Serves 4 as an appetizer.

Sesame & Sprout Spread

2 *tablespoons sesame paste*	1 *teaspoon vegetable salt*
¾ *cup tofu*	3 *teaspoons soy sauce*

1 *clove garlic, crushed (optional)*
1 *cup sprouts — chop if they're large*

Mash together everything except the sprouts to make a smooth paste. Mix in the sprouts. Makes about 1½ cups.

This spread is good on dark bread with tomato slices, on biscuits or as filling for celery sticks.

Mushroom Flan

1 *uncooked pie case*   1 *teaspoon grated onion*
1½ *cups sautéed sliced mushrooms seasoned salt*
2 *eggs*   *pepper to taste*
6 *oz. yogurt*

Cook the pie case in a 400°F. oven for 10 minutes. Reduce heat to 325°F.

Spread the mushrooms in the pie case. Beat together the eggs, yogurt, onion, ½ teaspoon salt and pepper. Sprinkle the mushrooms with a little seasoned salt and pour the egg mixture over them.

Bake at 325°F. for about 40 minutes or until lightly browned. Let cool. Chill.

Cut in small wedges to serve.

Tomato Ice

½ *pint tomato sauce*   2 *tablespoons lemon juice*
1 *clove garlic, crushed*   3 *slices fresh ginger*
1 *onion, sliced*   1 *teaspoon Worcestershire sauce*
1 *leafy stalk celery, sliced* ½ *teaspoon cayenne pepper*
1 *carrot, sliced*   1 *egg white*
1 *tablespoon soy sauce*
1 *teaspoon fresh lemon rind*

Heat together the tomato sauce, garlic, onion, celery, carrot, soy sauce, lemon rind and juice, and ginger. Bring to a boil, cover and simmer 10 minutes. Press the mixture through a fine sieve.

Allow to cool. Stir in the Worcestershire sauce and cayenne.

Place the mixture in an ice cube tray or metal pan and freeze, covered, until almost firm. Scoop the mixture into a bowl and beat with a wire whisk to break up any icy crystals. Beat the egg white to stiff peaks and stir it into the tomato mixture. Freeze until almost firm, then whisk as before. Return to the freezer for about an hour before serving.

To serve, layer in parfait glasses with thinly sliced cucumber, or place a scoop in a chilled avocado half.

Serves 6.

Chickpea Snacks

2 *cups cooked chickpeas*
$\frac{1}{2}$ *cup peanut oil*
1 *clove garlic, crushed*
1 *small onion, minced*
1$\frac{1}{2}$ *teaspoons salt*
1 *teaspoon oregano*
2 *teaspoons parsley*
juice of $\frac{1}{2}$ *lemon*

Drain the chickpeas well. Heat the oil and add the chickpeas and cook them for about 10 minutes over low heat. Add all of the remaining ingredients. Cook for 10 minutes more, stirring occasionally. The peas should brown slightly. Remove the peas and drain them.

Serve warm or cold as an appetizer, snack, or salad ingredient.

Walnut Pinecone

1 *oz. crumbled blue cheese*
1 *cup homemade cottage cheese, lightly packed*
1 *teaspoon grated onion*
1 *tablespoon yogurt*
walnuts

Mix cheeses, onion and yogurt. Mix and mash until quite smooth. Mould into pinecone shape and refrigerate for at least 2 hours.

Garnish cheese mound with walnuts to resemble a pinecone. Serve with SESAME WAFERS (see page   ).

Our homemade cottage cheese is quite dry, so if you will be using "store" cheese, drain it first.

Pumpkinseed Pinecone

8 *oz. finely grated sharp ched-*   ¼ *teaspoon paprika*
   dar cheese   1 *teaspoon caraway seeds*
4 *tablespoons yogurt*   *pumpkin seeds*
½ *teaspoon dry mustard*

Mix and mash together everything except pumpkin seeds, until quite smooth. Form into pinecone shape. Chill for at least 2 hours.

Garnish chilled mound with pumpkin seeds to resemble a pinecone. Serve with SESAME WAFERS (see page 174).

Spiced Peanuts
(*Try not to eat them all up while you make them.*)

1 *lb. raw peanuts with skins on*   2 *teaspoons chili powder*
2 *fl. oz. vegetable oil*   ½ *teaspoon hot paprika*
2 *cloves garlic, chopped*   ½ *teaspoon cumin powder*

Heat oven to 300°F.

Spread peanuts in roasting pan. Toast at 300°F. for 25 minutes, stirring occasionally.

Meanwhile, heat oil and cook garlic gently for about 10 minutes but do not let it brown. Strain oil and mix with spices and salt.

Pour spiced oil over peanuts and toss to mix well. Roast spiced nuts for 20 minutes more, stirring occasionally.

Drain nuts on absorbent paper. Let cool before storing in airtight containers.

Lunchbox Favourites

For those of us who are concerned about nutrition, eliminating "junk foods," etc., lunches are often the most difficult meal of the day. Meals offered by schools are usually planned by competent dieticians, but no one can promise that your child will eat all the vegetables and forego the white-bread-with-margarine and the imitation vanilla flavoured, sugar-filled ice cream. Adults who can not eat lunch at home are faced with the alternatives of crowded, expensive restaurants or "fast-food" lunches that are a nutritional and gastronomic disaster. A return to the old-fashioned lunchbox may be the answer. However, stuffing one or more lunchboxes every day with wholesome, interesting, tasty food can be a problem. Unless there is a certain amount of planning, it can become a chore and a great temptation to succumb to "convenience" foods. Actually, with a little planning, you can make your *own* convenience foods. After all, if you're packing several lunches every morning, you need all the convenience you can get!

First, you need the right equipment. Buy a lunchbox that will hold what you need. Most lunchboxes come equipped with a thermos, but you will need space for at least one more small (about 4 pint), widemouth thermos. If you want to carry soup or a stew for lunch, you will have to choose between taking a beverage in your large thermos or finding a space for a second one.

Your next item is staples. If you are not inclined to produce enough homemade bread, you'll find a variety of very good whole grain breads ready-made. Many shops also carry frozen sandwich meats and frozen vegetarian "meats" which are free from sodium nitrate and nitrite.

Natural cheeses, soy snacks, sunflower seeds, pumpkin seeds, even corn chips and pickles are other staples for lunchboxes to be found in your health food store. Dried fruits are great for "dessert," and if you are lucky, you may also find fresh, unsprayed, unwaxed, ungassed fruits and vegetables.

Planning is constant. Your evening meal should be planned, if possible, to produce goodies for the lunchbox. Every roast should provide slices for sandwiches. The slices can be frozen in individual portions until needed. Make an *extra* meatloaf, cool, slice and freeze in individual portions. If your family has favourite soups, stews or casseroles, make enough extra to fill the thermos. We also keep a supply of cheap, stainless steel forks and spoons. They can be reused indefinitely, and they're not so valuable that you have to worry about smaller children losing them. Fruit salads, potato salads, bean salads, etc. can provide lunchbox fare, too. The small thermoses are ideal for packing these items.

With just a little effort, your lunchbox can be a mini-lesson in economy and ecology. The thermoses, of course, are reusable, as is the stainless steel cutlery. Invest in bright coloured, washable cloth napkins, and use them instead of paper. Washing them is less costly and less wasteful than the constant one-time use of paper napkins.

Here are some of our lunchbox favourites:

Beverages:
Fruit juice
Yogurt drinks
Hot or cold herb teas
Hot or cold carob milk

Large Wide-mouth Thermos:
Soups, hot or cold
Stews
Casseroles

Small Wide-mouth Thermos:
Cottage cheese, vary with chopped vegetables or fruit

Fruit or vegetable salads
Yogurt
Rice pudding
Chopped fruit with coconut shreds
Dried fruit compote

Miscellaneous Goodies:
Carrot, cucumber or celery sticks
Homemade cookies, scones, etc.
Nuts
Cheese cubes
Olives
Cherry tomatoes
Dried fruit
Fresh fruit
Soybean snacks
Crisps (from your health food store)
Wholegrain biscuits and flatbreads
Chewable protein wafers
Chewable Vitamin C tablets
Edible dried seaweed (dulse, nori, etc.)
Seeds
Sandwiches

Soups from Avgolemono to Zuppa

Soup is much more than just a liquid with which to begin a meal. It is a food and should be the epitome of fine flavour and nutrition.

Nearly every region and nationality has a soup whose aromas and flavours will always evoke "home." Potato soup, bean soup, onion soup, chicken soup — very simple — but spiced with the joys and dreams of remembered childhood. Soup is the traditional healer for the sick, sustainer for the bereaved, invalid's potion and nourishment for the cold and hungry. Tinned and instant soup manufacturers have taken lucrative cognizance of the emotional satisfaction we find in soup.

Soup is also a convenience food. Homemade soup can usually be "put together" in less than an hour and will provide a hearty and nutritious meal. Stock, of course, takes quite a long time to cook but you don't have to hover over it, stir it or pay much attention to the timing. Furthermore, stock may be made in large quantities to be stored in the refrigerator or freezer, to be used as needed. If you haven't any stock, vegetable cooking water is a handy substitute. Boiling potatoes, for instance, requires a quantity of water. While the potatoes cook, some of the nutrients and flavour are lost in the cooking water. If the water is discarded, they are truly lost. Using the cooking water for soup is good for your health, your purse and the ecology! Just remember that vegetable cooking water comes in a great range of flavours, from the bland flavour of potato to the strong flavour of broccoli and other cabbages.

Not many years ago, there was a widely publicized mythical beast called "leftover soup." The idea is that you would scrape food scraps into a simmering pot on the back of the stove where all the flavours would magically blend into a delicious soup. Furthermore, the myth continued, the longer you left the "soup" to cook and the more you added, the better it would be. While it is true that leftover cooked bones and meat scraps can flavour a stock, cooked vegetables have nothing much to offer — and when you add the indiscriminate potpourri of sauces, herbs, spices and condiments — no, thank you!

One essential fact, with which the soup manufacturers seem unable to cope, is that when you eat soup, you should be able to taste the ingredients. The flavours may be blended, but they shouldn't be blurred beyond recognition. Soup should be cooked until the main ingredient is done — no longer. It is *stock* which simmers all day, *not soup*.

Stock

Stock is a liquid flavoured by the extraction of the vitamins, minerals, taste and colour of meat, bones, fish, vegetables and seasonings. The extraction requires long, slow cooking, after which the ingredients will have become mushy, pale and flavourless and the stock rich and tasty. The stock is then used as a liquid in which other ingredients are cooked *but only until they are done.* Thus you will have the tasty stock and the flavourful ingredients enhancing one another.

We make our stocks with little or no salt because it simplifies later seasoning. You may want to "stretch" a soup with more stock but if both are already salted, you may get a briny brew, indeed.

There are as many "proper" ways to make stock as there are cooks. Beef stock, for instance, may be made with or without vegetables, brown the bones or not, add this herb or that. You may add flour or not. In other words, stock is just what you want it to be. Added to stews and casseroles as well as soups, it is that "something extra" that can make a good dish great. You can also make a more concentrated stock by boiling the finished stock hard until the quantity is reduced by about half, but we seldom find this necessary.

When making beef, chicken, or veal stock, be sure to add a little wine or vinegar to extract some of the calcium from the bones.

Basic Brown Beef Stock

2–3 *lbs. meaty bones (about ⅓ meat)*
1 *onion, cut in chunks*
1 *carrot, cut in chunks*
1 *additional lb. meaty bones, including marrow bones, if possible*
1 *whole onion, stuck with a clove*
2 *cloves garlic*
10 *peppercorns*
1 *whole carrot*
1 *bay leaf*
½ *cup red wine or sherry* or ¼ *cup vinegar*

Place the 2–3 lbs. bone, the chunked carrot and the chunked onion in a heavy ovenproof pan. (We use a black iron skillet.) Let brown in a 400°F. oven for 30 minutes. Transfer the bones and vegetables to a large kettle. Add about one cup of water to the ovenproof pan and scrape up all the browned bits.

Add the water with the browned bits to the kettle. Add all the remaining ingredients and enough water to cover it all generously. Bring to a boil, skim, lower the heat and simmer for three to four hours. Strain the stock. Save the marrow to spread on bread, if you like it, but nothing else is worth saving. The stock will keep about five days in the refrigerator or six months in the freezer.

Leftover cooked bones and meat may be used as part of the meat in Beef Stock but for the best flavour, you need some fresh bones and meat as well.

Basic Veal Stock

2–3 *lbs. meaty bones*	1 *small bay leaf*
1 *onion*	5 *peppercorns*
1 *carrot*	$\frac{1}{2}$ *cup sherry* or
1 *stalk celery*	$\frac{1}{4}$ *cup vinegar*

Put all ingredients into a large kettle and add enough water to cover generously. Bring to a boil, skim, reduce heat and let simmer for three to four hours. Strain the stock.

Chicken Stock

a fat old hen, about 2 *lbs.*	1 *onion*
2 *carrots*	1 *bay leaf*
1 *leafy stalk celery*	$\frac{1}{4}$ *cup white wine*

Wash the hen and put it in a large pot with water to cover. Add the carrots, celery and onion. Bring to a full boil, reduce the heat to simmer and let cook for two hours. Add the bay leaf and cook 30 minutes more.

Skim the soup, strain the broth. This is a good, strong broth.

Remove the meat from the chicken and put the skin into a pot. Crack the large bones and add all the bones to the pot with the skin. Add about a quart of water and fresh vegetables, as above. Simmer for about 45 minutes to make a weaker broth than the first, but one which will still add flavour to cooking.

Use the chicken meat in soups. Most of the flavour has been cooked out, so it's not very good for salads or sandwiches.

Fish Stock

2 *lbs. fish, including heads*   1 *bay leaf*
  and bones $\frac{1}{2}$ *lemon, sliced*
1 *onion, cut in chunks*   *pinch salt*
1 *carrot, cut in chunks*   6 *fl. oz. white wine*
1 *leafy stalk celery, cut in*
  chunks

Put all ingredients in a large pot. Add water to cover generously.

Bring to a boil, skim, lower heat and simmer one and one half hours. Strain.

Vegetarian Stock

1 *clove garlic, cracked*   1 *tablespoon brewers' yeast*
1 *carrot, sliced*   4 *cups water*
1 *stalk celery, with leaves,*   1 *bay leaf*
  sliced   1 *tablespoon chopped parsley*
3 *tablespoons vegetable oil*   *thyme and marjoram – a gener-*
2 *tablespoons whole wheat*   *ous pinch of each*
  flour

Wilt the garlic, carrot, onion and celery in the oil until just translucent. Stir in the flour and the yeast. Add the water gradually, stirring constantly. Add the bay leaf and herbs and simmer 30 minutes. Strain the broth.

Makes about $2\frac{1}{2}$ cups.

You may make a darker stock by browning the vegetables lightly before adding the flour.

Iced Cucumber Soup

2 cucumbers	1 tablespoon minced parsley
4 spring onions	1 cup sour cream or 1 cup
1 tablespoon vegetable oil	yogurt or ½ cup of each
3 cups vegetable cooking water	salt to taste

Dice one cucumber. Chop the spring onions. Sauté them in the oil until they begin to be translucent, add the cucumber, stir briefly, add the vegetable water and simmer, covered 10 minutes or until cucumber is very soft. Add the parsley to the broth and purée the mixture in the blender. Seed the remaining cucumber. Grate it into the purée. Let cool to lukewarm. Stir in the sour cream or yogurt. Add salt to taste. Chill. Serve cold.
Serves 4.

Sprouty Egg Flower Soup

6 cups rich chicken broth	1 spring onion, finely minced
1 cup bean sprouts	½ cup minced green sprouts
2 eggs, lightly beaten	(alfalfa, mustard or cress)

Heat the chicken broth to boiling. Add the bean sprouts. Stir the boiling soup and while stirring, add the egg. Remove the soup from the heat immediately and garnish with the spring onion and minced green sprouts. Serve hot.
Serves 6.

Avgolemono
A Wonderful Greek variation of chicken soup

3 pints good flavoured chicken stock	3 whole eggs plus 1 egg yolk
½ cup raw long-grain brown rice	juice of 2 lemons

Bring broth to a boil and add rice. Cook about 30 minutes or until rice is tender. Remove from heat and keep warm.

Beat eggs and yolk with a wire whisk until frothy and lemon-coloured. Beat in lemon juice. Add two cups of hot chicken broth to egg mixture, whisking constantly.

Add egg mixture to remaining soup, whisking constantly. The soup may be heated almost to the boiling point but if it boils the eggs will curdle.

Serve hot.
Serves 8.

Avocado Velvet
A quick, easy, delicious soup

2 avocadoes, peeled, seeded and sliced	2 spring onions, chopped
1 cup potato cooking water	½ teaspoon salt
	1 cup yogurt

Blend the avocadoes, potato water, spring onions and salt. Place in a pretty bowl and fold in the yogurt.
Serves 4.

Icy Apple Soup

2 apples, cored and finely chopped	⅔ cup apple juice
1 cup water	½ cup plain yogurt
	cinnamon

Simmer the apples in the water for 10 minutes. Mash, blend or purée. Chill.

Lightly blend the chilled apple mixture with the juice and yogurt. Chill well. Serve with a sprinkle of cinnamon.
Serves 2.

Cock-a-Leeky Soup
A family favourite from Scotland

1 *chicken – not too young (about 4 lbs.)*	½ *teaspoon white pepper*
2 *teaspoons salt*	1 *cup brown rice*
	6–10 *leeks*

Place chicken in a large pot, add 5 pints of water, salt and pepper and cook chicken just until it is tender. Cooking time will depend on the bird's size and weight. Remove the cooked chicken from the pot.

Add rice to stock and simmer 20 minutes.

While rice cooks, wash leeks carefully, cut off and discard the tough green part and shred the white part finely. Shred the chicken meat. Save the bones and skin to make a broth (see CHICKEN STOCK recipe page 30).

Add shredded leeks to simmering stock and cook 10 minutes more. Add shredded chicken meat and let heat through. Serve hot.

Serves 8.

Turkeybone Soup
We think it's the best part of the bird!

bones and skin from a roast turkey	1–2 *onions*
	whole wheat pasta
1–2 *stalks celery with leaves*	*salt and pepper to taste*

Disjoint bones as much as possible and place in large pan. Add skin but save any meat scraps for later. Add cold water to cover bones by several inches. Bring to a boil, reduce heat and let simmer for about two hours.

Dice celery and onion finely.

Strain stock into a large pot. Add chopped celery and onion and cook in stock until well done. Add pasta and cook until done.

Meanwhile, strip any excess meat from cooked bones. Dice the meat small and dice any other left-over turkey to

match. Stir diced meat into stock. Add salt and pepper to
taste.
Serves 8.

Basic Vegetable Beef Soup

½ lb. or more beef, any cut,   ½ cup fresh or frozen peas
   diced in ½ inch pieces   2 medium size potatoes, diced
pinch salt   ½ to 1 cup whole wheat elbow
2½ pints beef stock   macaroni or noodles
1 carrot, diced   salt and pepper to taste
1 leek diced (white part only)

Put diced beef in a pot with water to cover, add a pinch of
salt and simmer gently until beef is cooked through (about
20 minutes). Add the stock, carrot, leek, peas and potatoes. Bring to a boil and add macaroni. Cook until
macaroni is done, about 12 minutes. Taste for seasoning.
    Vary the vegetables to suit your fancy. Whatever is in
season is best.
Serves 6.

Basic Vegetable Soup

½ cup barley   2½ cups vegetarian stock
4 cups diced fresh vegetables   salt and pepper to taste

Cook barley in five cups of boiling water 20 minutes or
until done. While water is still boiling, drop vegetables in
a little at a time. Simmer 10 minutes or until vegetables
are done. Add stock and cook just to heat through. Taste
for seasoning.
    This soup can be made with almost any vegetables in
infinite combinations. Any grain or pasta may replace the
barley. Fresh herbs can offer even more variety.
Serves 6.

Mushroom Soup

1 lb. mushrooms
2 tablespoons vegetable oil
1 med. onion, chopped
2 tablespoons whole wheat flour
2 cups vegetable stock
3 cups water from cooking vegetables

salt and pepper to taste
3 tablespoons bulghur
1 bay leaf
2 tablespoons chopped water-cress, for garnish

Chop mushroom stems and slice caps.

Heat oil in a large frying-pan add onion and mushrooms and stir to mix well. Put the lid on *upside down* and allow mushrooms to "sweat" over lowest heat for five minutes. Stir in flour. Add stock and water a little at a time, stirring constantly. Add salt and pepper, bulghur and bay leaf and simmer 15 to 20 minutes or until bulghur is done. Remove bay leaf. Serve hot, garnished with watercress.

Serves 6.

Peanut Soup

An up-dated, high-protein version of a recipe from colonial Virginia.

1 medium onion, chopped finely
1 stalk celery, chopped finely
3 tablespoons oil
2 tablespoons whole wheat flour

2 cups chicken or turkey stock or vegetable cooking water
1 cup smooth, unsalted peanut butter
32 fl.oz. yogurt
salt to taste

Chop onion and celery together. Heat oil in heavy five-pint pan. Sauté onion and celery until translucent. Stir in flour; add stock and bring to a boil. Using a wire whisk, stir in peanut butter and blend until smooth. Stir in yogurt. Add salt to taste.

Serve hot or cold.

Serves 6.

Pumpkin Soup

1 *small onion, chopped fine*   *8 fl. oz. light cream or yogurt*
1 *tablespoon oil*   *salt to taste*
1¼ *pints milk*
2½ *cups pumpkin purée, see page* 73

Heat oil and sauté onion until just translucent. Stir in milk and heat gently until milk is heated through. With a wire whisk, stir in pumpkin purée, stirring until smooth. Heat through. Add cream or yogurt and salt to taste.
   Serves 4.

More Pumpkin Soups

To the finished pumpkin soup, add:
1 *tablespoon chili powder*   *OR*
OR   1 *teaspoon of your favourite*
1 *tablespoon curry powder*   *herb, finely chopped (½ teas-*
                                     poon dried)

Plain Potato Soup
To make this into fancy potato soup, also known as Vichysoisse, we'd have to peel the potatoes!

2 *lbs. potatoes, UNpeeled, cut*   1½ *pints chicken stock*
   up   *dash white pepper*
1 *carrot, sliced*   2 *teaspoons salt*
2 *leeks, white part only, sliced* 1½ *pints milk*

Cook all ingredients except milk together for 25 minutes. Purée through a sieve or blend. Add milk. Serve hot or cold.
   You may increase the number of leeks, use yogurt in place of some of the milk, garnish the soup with fresh chopped chives or parsley — even substitute an onion for

the leeks (one onion equals two leeks).

We also like it with two tablespoons of fresh dill, chopped and added to the soup just before serving.

Serves 8.

Cream of Fresh Tomato Soup

Here is a soup we enjoy when the tomatoes are ripe. Freeze to savour all winter.

2 *cups chopped, ripe tomatoes*
1 *medium onion, chopped*
1 *small clove garlic, squished through a press*
½ *teaspoon salt*
tiny pinch allspice
1 *oz butter*

2 *tablespoons whole wheat flour*
½ *pint milk*
½ *cup cream*
chopped fresh basil or dill as a garnish

Mix and mash the tomatoes, onion, garlic and salt. Simmer over low heat for about five minutes or until the onion is soft. Set aside.

Melt the butter in a large, heavy pan. Stir in the flour and cook very gently, stirring for three minutes. Add the milk and blend well to make a smooth sauce. Strain the tomato mixture into the sauce through a sieve, mixing it well. Heat to boiling point. Stir in the cream. Garnish with basil or dill. Serve hot.

Serves 4.

Yogurt Soup

1 *cucumber*
¼ *cup fresh mint leaves (2 teaspoons dried)*
¼ *cup fresh parsley (2 teaspoons dried)*

1 *teaspoon olive oil*
1 *teaspoon honey*
8 *oz. yogurt*

Peel and seed the cucumber and cut it into very small pieces. Liquify everything in the blender. If you do not have a blender, grate the cucumber, then beat everything with a wire whisk until well blended. Chill about 1 hour. Makes 1½ cups.

Three small portions.

Winter Lentil Soup

6 *oz lentils*	1 *medium diced onion*
12 *fl. oz water*	1 *clove crushed garlic*
1 *medium potato*	¼ *teaspoon thyme*
1 *small turnip*	3 *tablespoons soy sauce*
1 *small carrot*	*salt and pepper to taste*

Cook lentils in water, covered for 25–30 minutes until tender but not mushy.

Meanwhile, dice potato, turnip and carrot. If they are organically grown and not paraffined, don't peel them. Put them in a pot with water to cover, cook about 10 minutes or until just tender.

Add lentils and their cooking water, if any, to diced vegetables and *their* cooking water. Add everything else and as much water as you like to make a fairly thick soup.

Serves 4.

Lentil Souper

6 *oz lentils*	2 *tablespoons sesame paste*
3 *cups water*	*(tahini)*
1 *carrot, sliced*	½ *cup water*
1 *small onion, diced*	1 *tablespoon brewers' yeast*
1 *clove garlic, crushed*	2 *tablespoons tomato paste*
¼ *teaspoon thyme*	*salt and pepper to taste*

Add the lentils to the water, bring to a boil and simmer for about 20 minutes. Add the remaining ingredients and

simmer 10 minutes more. Add a little water if the soup is too thick.
Serves 2.

Hearty Whole Grain Soup

2 *tablespoons oil*	½ *cup each millet, bulghur,*
1 *medium onion, diced*	*barley*
1 *medium carrot, diced*	2½ *pints water*
3 *cloves garlic, chopped finely*	*salt*
1 *leafy stalk celery, chopped*	*pepper*
finely	*thyme*
1 *green pepper, chopped finely*	

Heat the oil in a large pot and sauté the vegetables until the onion is translucent. Add the grains and mix well. Add the water and heat to boiling. Cover the pot and simmer 30 minutes. Season to taste with salt, pepper and thyme (just a pinch). Heat, taste and correct seasoning.
Serves 6–8.

Variations: Add chopped peeled tomatoes after the grains have cooked but before seasoning. Add a bunch of chopped fresh parsley just before serving. Add any cooked leftover vegetables. Season with soy sauce instead of salt. Use basil instead of thyme.

Black Bean Soup
The gourmet's bean soup

1 *lb. black (turtle) beans*	*dash red pepper (Cayenne)*
2 *stalks celery with leaves,*	1½ *teaspoons salt*
chopped finely	2 *tablespoons fresh lemon juice*
2 *large onions, chopped finely*	*sherry*
1 *sweet red or green pepper,*	1 *lemon, sliced very thinly*
seeded and chopped finely	

Wash beans thoroughly and soak in water to cover overnight.

Add enough water to soaked beans to cover generously.

Add celery, onions and pepper. *So not add salt or the beans might stay hard and never soften.* Cook beans until very soft, adding water as needed, about one and a half hours.

When beans are soft, add salt. Mash beans or purée in a blender to make a smooth soup. Stir in lemon juice. Serve hot, garnished with lemon slices.

Diners may add a tablespoon or two of sherry to their soup if they wish.

Serves 4–6.

Great Bean Soup

1 *lb. dried haricot beans*
3 *tablespoons vegetable oil*
3 *onions, chopped*
2 *carrots, chopped*
1 *large green or red pepper, seeded and chopped*

2 *cloves garlic, minced*
3 *large tomatoes, peeled, seeded and chopped*
2 *tablespoons molasses*
salt and pepper to taste

Soak beans overnight in water to cover. Cook until soft, about one and a half hours, but do not add any salt.

Heat vegetable oil in large pan. Gently sauté onions, carrots, pepper and garlic until onion is becoming translucent. Add tomatoes, molasses and cooked beans. Stir in enough water to make thick soup. Cook 30 minutes to blend all flavours. Add salt and pepper to taste and cook 10 minutes more. Serve hot.

This soup can be as thick or thin as you please but we like it just a bit thicker than a cream soup.

Try different types of beans for variety.

Serves 8.

Iced Curry Soup

2 *tablespoons oil*
1 *medium onion, chopped finely*
1 *tablespoon curry powder*
2 *tablespoons whole wheat flour*
2 *cups vegetable stock*
1 *teaspoon lemon peel*
juice of ½ *lemon*
1 *bay leaf*
1 *tablespoon cornflour, mixed with* 2 *tablespoons water*
16 *fl. oz. yogurt*

Heat the oil and sauté the onion until it is soft. Add the curry powder and mix well. Add the flour, and cook for a minute or two, stirring. Stir in the stock. Add the lemon peel, lemon juice and bay leaf. Simmer for 10 minutes. Thicken if needed with the cornflour and water. Chill thoroughly. Stir in the yogurt.
Serves 6.

Fish Soup with Rice

1½ *lbs. fish fillets*
fish heads and bones
2 *bay leaves*
2 *cloves garlic, cracked*
3 *tablespoons olive oil*
1 *medium onion, chopped*
1 *carrot, sliced*
1 *stalk celery, sliced*
1 *tomato, peeled and chopped*
3 *pints water*
½ *cup brown rice*
salt and pepper to taste

Wrap the fish fillets in cheesecloth. Wrap the fish heads and bones with the bay leaves and garlic in another piece of cheesecloth. Heat the olive oil in a large pot and sauté the onion until golden. Add the carrot, celery, tomato and water and bring to a boil. Add the fish. Simmer for one hour, removing the fillets when they are tender. Time will depend on size and coarseness of the fish. Skim the pot as needed. Remove the fish and bones from the pot and set aside. Add the rice and simmer ½ hour or until rice is cooked. Flake the fish fillets and return the flakes to the pot. Season to taste with salt and pepper.
Serves 4–6.

Cream of Chestnut Soup

1½ lbs. fresh chestnuts, skinned
1½ pints chicken stock
2 oz butter
2 medium onions, chopped

2 leafy stalks celery, chopped
1 cup milk (about)
salt and cayenne pepper to taste

Place chestnuts in large pot and just cover with stock. (Set remaining stock aside). Add 1 oz. butter. Bring to a boil, cover and simmer 30 minutes.

Heat the remaining 1 oz. butter and sauté the onion and celery until soft. Add remaining stock, cover and simmer 10 minutes. Strain the stock and discard the vegetables.

Purée the cooked chestnuts in a blender or sieve, adding the stock as needed. Mix the chestnut purée with any remaining stock and enough milk to make a thick, creamy soup. Season to taste.

Serves 4.

Soy-Tomato Soup

2 tablespoons oil
1 onion, cut up
1½ cups tomatoes, peeled, seeded and chopped
½ teaspoon rosemary

2 cups cooked soybeans
2 tablespoons brewers' yeast
2 cups water
¼ cup soy sauce

Heat oil and sauté onion until translucent. Add tomatoes and simmer 2–3 minutes. Add all remaining ingredients and bring to a boil.

Serves 4.

Sunflower Soup

1 *carrot, sliced*
1 *leafy stalk celery, sliced*
1 *medium onion, sliced*
1 *clove garlic, quartered*
2 *tablespoons brewers' yeast*
2 *tablespoons tomato paste*

generous   pinch   saffron
   (optional)
3 *cups water*
1 *cup sunflower seeds, hulled*
½ *cup soy sauce*
chopped chives

Place the carrot, celery, onion, garlic, yeast, tomato paste, saffron and water in a pot and bring to a boil. Cover the pot and simmer for 30 minutes over low heat. Remove from heat and let cool slightly. Pulverize the sunflower seeds in a blender. Add the sunflower flour to the cooked soup and purée all ingredients until smooth. Stir in the soy sauce. Add enough water to make 4 cups of soup (or thin to taste). Heat the soup thoroughly. Garnish with the chopped chives.
    Serves 4.

Chicken Noodle Soup

1½ *pints chicken stock*
2 *carrots, sliced*
1 *onion, diced*
1 *stalk celery, diced*
1 *tablespoon parsley, minced*

½ *cup fresh or frozen peas*
½ *cup chopped cooked chicken*
½ *cup whole wheat noodles (not*
   cooked)
salt and pepper to taste

Heat the stock and add the carrots, onion, celery and parsley. Simmer, covered for 20 minutes. Add the peas, chicken and noodles. Cover the pot and simmer about 10 minutes or until the noodles are cooked. Add water if needed. Add salt and pepper to taste.
    Serves 4–6.

Kale Soup

4 tablespoons oil
1 medium onion, chopped
1 clove garlic, crushed
½ lb. fresh kale, washed and
   shredded
2 tablespoons bran
1 cup water
2 tablespoons soy sauce

2 tablespoons whole wheat
   flour
1 tablespoon brewers' yeast
1 cup milk or water
½ teaspoon basil
¼ teaspoon cinnamon
salt to taste

Heat 2 tablespoons oil in a large frying pan. Add the onion, garlic and kale, and stir over moderate heat until the kale is wilted. Add the bran, 1 cup water and soy sauce. Cover the pan and steam 5 minutes. Let cool slightly, then purée in a blender.

Heat the remaining 2 tablespoons oil in a large saucepan. Add the flour and yeast and mix well. Stir in the milk and cook 2–3 minutes, stirring. Add the kale purée and the seasonings. Heat through.

Serves 4.

Salad Days

The best place to eat a salad is in the garden. The farther a food is from its natural habitat, the less likely it is to be good to eat. Every moment between picking and eating means a loss of quality. We take it for granted that processing causes a reduction of nutrients but we tend to think of processing as including only such things as freezing, tinning, mixing and freeze-drying. Shipping, storing and distribution are also processes and during these the quality of fresh food is damaged. Even the washing and handling of fresh garden vegetables destroys valuable nutrients.

Essential to an appreciation of the factors which affect the quality of food is an understanding of what causes spoilage. The fresh vegetables you buy in a supermarket aren't spoiled but spoilage has begun and will continue until it is stopped by heat, cold or being eaten.

One of the major factors in spoilage is the action of enzymes. Enzymes are catalysts which contribute to the growth, ripening and manufacture of vitamins within plants. When the plant has fully ripened, the enzymes keep working, helping to break down the plant material, speeding the process of decay. The human body manufactures its own enzymes, which are essential to the digestive process. Our own enzymes, and those we get from the raw foods we eat, function in a wide temperature range, roughly between 40°F. and 200°F. Refrigeration slows them down but doesn't stop them entirely. Failure to blanch vegetables properly before they are frozen results in a loss of colour, texture and taste because the enzymes aren't stopped soon enough. Enzymes reactivate as foods thaw, and for this reason, food should be cooked frozen or as soon as thawed and cannot be successfully re-frozen. At room temperature enzymes are positively rampant! And it is at room temperature that most of the damage to fresh produce occurs.

Even picking your own good, garden vegetables may require a little planning. I tend to stroll and dream in the garden, noticing and admiring all the new buds, plants and ripening things. Unless I'm out picking kale or turnips or anything else on a cold day in January, I have to start my stroll at the end of the garden farthest from my eventual objective. The last thing I do is pick the thing I came after. Then it goes straight to the refrigerator, or better yet, we eat it after a very quick rinse in cool water.

There is a good reason for rinsing vegetables quickly. Water is another factor which robs foods of valuable nutrients. Many vitamins and minerals are water soluble. Boiling is a terrible way to treat vegetables but at least you can save the broth and use it in cooking. Soaking away vitamins and minerals is sheer waste! Don't wash vegetables and fruits until you are ready to use them and then wash them very quickly in cool water and dry immediately. Wire salad baskets are great for drying greens. Fill one with wet greens, swing it in a circle and let centrifugal force send the water flying. (Do it outdoors.) Greens may also be dried by patting with terry towels, which is a little time-consuming, but an inventive friend puts her greens in a pillowcase and swings it like a wire basket.

Light and oxygen are two more enemies in the battle to save vitamins and minerals. Enzymes need light and air in order to destroy some nutrients. Produce should be closely wrapped and kept in a dark refrigerator.

Now that we have the ingredients for our salad, let's talk about *why* salads are so great. For one thing, *heat* is another destroyer of vitamins and minerals. Fresh, raw vegetables are not only more nutritious than cooked — most of them taste better. Carrots are a good example. They are lovely when properly cooked, but very different from fresh raw carrots. Celery is another vegetable whose character changes drastically when cooked. Raw spinach is one of the most delicious salad greens imaginable. Raw spinach also has about twice the magnesium of cooked; more than half again as much protein; more calcium; phosphorous; iron, sodium and potassium; more Vitamin A; thiamine; riboflavin; niacin; and almost *four times* more Vitamin C! Spinach is a typical example. In some cases cooking enhances the palatability and even digestibility of a vegetable but most are better raw. Those that aren't actually *better* are still surprisingly good. Walking through the asparagus patch with a friend in early spring, I broke off two young stalks, handed one to my friend and bit into the other. My friend was sceptical — until she took her first bite — then she became a convert to the joys of *raw* asparagus. If you haven't tried raw turnips, beetroots, broccoli, cauliflower, courgettes, peas, stringbeans, etc., you should. They're delicious!

Why not just eat the vegetables raw then? Why go to all the trouble of concocting a salad? First, salads are more exciting. Raw cabbage is very good. Coleslaw is great. Second, you can get all kinds of nutritional bonuses in salads. Salads would be valuable for the oil alone (raw and cold-pressed, of course). Vinegar is rich in potassium, and Vitamin C-rich lemon juice is a delicious alternative. Vegetables and dressing are only the beginning. Consider sprouts, raw mushrooms, seeds, nuts, herbs, cheese, fruits and wheat germ. What about eggs, cooked meats and fish? There are olives of many tastes and colours, capers, croutons, seaweeds, cooked beans, rice and pasta. What a colourful palette for an inventive cook!

Any salad is only as good as its ingredients. We've talked about vegetables and freshness, let's talk about dressings and freshness. Raw, unrefined, cold-pressed oils come in a great variety of flavours and saturation. They can become rancid, though, so they should be kept re-frigerated after opening. Safflower oil, a light-flavoured polyunsaturate, is a very good salad oil. Soy, peanut and sunflower oils are very good, too. We use olive oil sparing-ly, because it is fairly saturated, but we don't want to give up its sunny flavour. Raw oils may have strong, distinctive flavours but they are available in bottles of varied sizes. Try an unfamiliar variety in small quantity. Most raw oils break down at relatively low temperatures (they begin to smoke) and are better used in salads than in frying. If you should happen to find an oil that is not your favourite for salads, use it in baking. Oils can be combined to provide even more variety.

Bottled dressings are boring. They are also a mind-boggling collection of thickeners, stabilizers, emulsifiers, preservatives and flavourings. Homemade dressings are never boring. At least they shouldn't be. There are as many combinations for dressings as there are ingredients for salads. Do give homemade mayonnaise a try. It's easy, delicious and you can vary the taste in many ways. There are many interesting, wholesome dressings available in your health food store as well.

The only really essential utensil for salad making is a container large enough to hold all of the ingredients. A long handled spoon and fork make salad mixing easier and a wire salad basket is a reliable and easy way to dry greens. A garlic press can be useful and a mortar and pestle are lovely for mashing herbs for dressings.

Salad recipes, more than most, should be patterns, mere guidelines which can — and should — be improvised upon. We are suggesting a few ideas, themes and variations. Let your imagination run free.

Basic Blue Cheese Dressing

3 *oz. very good fresh blue
  cheese*
2 *fl. oz oil*
2 *tablespoons fresh lemon juice*

Crumble all of the cheese, except one or two tablespoon-
fuls, over the salad. (This is very good on a salad of cos
lettuce and spinach with cucumber.) Add the oil to the
salad and toss to mix well. Mash the reserved cheese with
the lemon juice until it is thick and creamy — not
necessarily smooth — add the mixture to the salad and
toss to mix well.

Cucumber-cheese Mousse

2 *cucumbers, peeled, seeded
  and grated*
salt
4 *oz. cottage cheese*
1 *tablespoon minced chives*
¼ *teaspoon chopped fresh basil*

4 *fl. oz. plain yogurt*
salt and pepper to taste
1 *bar* (kanten) *agar-agar*
½ *pint water*
1 *tablespoon cider or wine
  vinegar*

Sprinkle the cucumbers with salt and press between two
plates for 10 minutes. Drain and rinse with cold water.
  Oil a ring mould.
  Mix the rinsed cucumbers with the cottage cheese,
chives, basil, yogurt and salt and pepper to taste. Chill.
  Break the agar-agar into the water and soak 20 minutes.
Cook in the water over low heat for about 10 minutes. Let
cool slightly. Add the vinegar. Stir in 1–2 tablespoons of
the cucumber mixture. Blend the agar-agar into the
cucumber mixture. Blend gently but thoroughly. Put
mixture into the mould and chill.
  To serve, dip the mould briefly into hot water (don't get
water in the mousse) and loosen the mousse with a knife
and turn onto a chilled plate. Garnish with parsley or
watercress.
  Serves 4–6.

Mixed Salad with Soy/Yogurt Dressing

½ *cup watercress*
1 *cup torn lettuce*
1 *tomato, chopped*
1 *cup coarsely chopped cabbage*
2 *carrots, shredded*

2 *spring onions, chopped*
1 *green pepper, chopped*
1 *oz. coarsely chopped cashews*
2 *oz. grated cheddar cheese*

Toss all ingredients together
  Makes 4 portions.

Soy/Yogurt Dressing

8 *oz. plain yogurt*
1 *oz soy flour*

2 *fl. oz cider vinegar*
herbs and spices to taste

Mix all dressing ingredients together.

Simple Salad Dressing

2½ *fl. oz. safflower oil*
2 *tablespoons fresh lemon juice*

Mix well. If the dressing is used on a salad for four, the dressing will supply for each person:

Calories 116
Fat 184 grams

Vitamin C 5% RDA
Iron 13% RDA

This dressing may be enhanced with the addition of fresh chopped herbs, kelp, crushed garlic, etc.

Tomato Aspic

1½ *pints tomato juice*
1 *packet agar-agar*
1 *celery stalk, cut up*
1 *onion, chopped*
1 *carrot, chopped*

juice of ½ lemon
2 *sprigs parsley*
1 *sprig basil*
pinch cinnamon

Soak the agar-agar in the tomato juice until soft. Add all the other ingredients and simmer, covered, 20 minutes. Strain. Let cool slightly. Pour into oiled mould and chill until set.

Unmould the aspic.

Serves 4.

Basic French Dressing with Green Salad

2½ *fl. oz. oil*
2 *tablespoons fresh lemon juice*
  or cider vinegar
½ *lb. salad greens (approx.)*

Rinse and dry greens. Tear them into a large salad bowl. Pour oil over greens and toss to mix well. Add lemon juice or vinegar. Toss and serve.

Variations: Add cracked garlic to the oil and let it stay there at least 8 hours. We keep a bottle of this garlic oil on hand.

Add chopped fresh or dried herbs to the lemon juice.

Add toasted sesame seeds after the oil.

Add sunflower seeds, sliced fresh mushrooms, grated cheese or fresh sprouts — or any combination — after the oil.

Add sliced raw beetroot, turnips, carrots, radishes, celery, tomatoes, cucumbers, peppers, broccoli florets, cauliflower florets, onions, shallots, spring onions, etc. *before* the oil.

Curry Dressing

2 *eggs*
1 *tablespoon honey*
1 *tablespoon cornflour*
½ *teaspoon powdered mustard*

¼ *teaspoon paprika*
1 *tablespoon curry powder*
⅓ *cup cider vinegar*
¾ *cup milk*

Beat eggs. Add honey, cornflour, mustard, paprika and curry powder. Mix well. Add vinegar and milk. Beat. Stir mixture over low heat until it thickens. Let cool.

Makes about one cup.

Yogurt Salad Dressing

1 *small carton yogurt*
1 *tsp lemon juice*
freshly chopped herbs such as
  chives, dill, thyme, basil,
  oregano — as much as you
  like of your favourites

1 *clove garlic, squished*
  through a press (optional)

Mix everything together and toss with your favourite salad.

Classic Caesar Salad

1 *glove garlic, crushed*
¼ *cup olive oil*
½ *cup safflower oil*
3 *slices whole wheat bread*
2 *eggs*
1 *tin anchovies (optional)*

2 *medium-sized heads cos lettuce*
2 *tablespoons fresh lemon juice*
½ *cup freshly grated Parmesan cheese*
freshly ground pepper

Add garlic to olive oil. Mix in safflower oil and let mixture stand overnight or at least 6 hours. Trim crusts from bread and cut into ½-inch cubes. Sauté bread cubes in ¼ cup of the garlic oil. Boil eggs for one minute, chill immediately and keep chilled.

If you use anchovies, drain oil and rinse anchovies under warm water to make them less salty.

Wash and dry the lettuce. Tear leaves into large bowl.

Add remaining ½ cup oil to the lettuce. Toss thoroughly. (At this point you can make a real production of the salad and bring all the ingredients to the table to finish.)

Break the eggs into the salad and toss to mix very well. Add lemon juice. Toss. Add the anchovies, bread cubes, cheese and pepper to taste. Toss with gusto. Serve with pride.

Serves 6–8

Potato Salad

4 *large baking potatoes*	3½ *tablespoons mayonnaise*
1 *teaspoon chopped parsley*	1 *tablespoon cider vinegar*
2 *tablespoons minced red onion*	
freshly ground black pepper to taste	

Cut potatoes in ½-inch dice and boil until just done — about 10 minutes. Drain potatoes and reserve cooking water for stock. Chill potatoes.

Toss chilled potatoes with parsley, onion and pepper. Add mayonnaise to potatoes and toss well. Add vinegar and toss to mix thoroughly.

Serves 4

Variations: Add chopped, hard-boiled eggs, chopped green pepper, crumbled crisp bacon, crumbled blue cheese, small cubes of sharp cheese, green or black olives.

Spinach and Mushroom Salad

½ *lb. fresh spinach*	⅓ *cup oil*
4–5 *large, fresh mushrooms*	2 *tablespoons lemon juice*
2 *hard-boiled eggs*	

Wash and dry spinach and tear into a large bowl. Wipe the mushrooms clean with a soft cloth and slice. Add to spinach. Peel eggs and halve them. Remove yolks and set them aside. Dice egg whites and add to the salad. Add oil,

toss. Add the lemon. Toss well. Top with egg yolks forced through a sieve.
Serves 4

Variations: Add 3 tablespoons sunflower seeds and 2 tablespoons wheat germ to the salad after the oil. Add ½ cup grated cheese before the oil.

Tropicale Salad

1 *large orange*	1 *tablespoon shredded raw*
2 *teaspoons minced red onion*	*coconut*
6–8 *leaves of salad greens*	½ *cup* Tropicale Dressing
3 *tablespoons sunflower seeds*	(see page 56)

Peel, seed and dice orange. Rinse and dry leaves. Tear leaves fairly small. Toss everything together.
Serves 4

Prawn Salad

½ *lb. freshly cooked peeled prawns*	1 *tablespoon minced watercress or salad cress*
1 *small cucumber*	1 *tablespoon minced chives*
1 *small, ripe tomato, seeded*	1 *tablespoon oil*
2 *tablespoons minced parsley*	1 *tablespoon fresh lemon juice*
	2 *hard-boiled eggs, peeled*

Seed cucumber and slice very thin. (Don't peel it unless it has been waxed.) Slice the tomato very thin. Add to prawns the cucumber, tomato, parsley, cress and chives. Toss to mix well. Add oil. Mix. Add lemon juice. Mix well. Serve garnished with slices of hard-boiled egg.
Makes 2 medium or 4 small portions.

Tropicale Dressing

3 *tablespoons honey*   1 *egg*
2 *tablespoons lime or lemon*   1 *small container yogurt*
  juice

In a small saucepan whisk together honey, lemon juice
and egg. Cook mixture, stirring, over medium heat until it
boils up frothy and thickens — about 10 minutes. Let cool.
When mixture is cool, stir in half of the yogurt and mix
well. Chill until serving time.
    Just before serving, fold in remaining yogurt.
    Makes about ½ pint.

Fruit Salad Tropicale

1 *apple*   ½ *cup raisins*
1 *banana*   ½ *cup fresh diced pineapple*
1 *orange*   ¼ *pint* Tropicale Dressing

Wash, core and dice apple. Peel, seed and dice orange.
Slice banana. Mix all ingredients together.
    Makes 2 large or 4 small portions.

Curried Cabbage Slaw

1 *small head cabbage, about* 1   1 *oz. fresh, raw grated coconut*
  lb., chopped fine   2 *teaspoons powdered sea kelp*
2 *oz. raisins*

Mix all the ingredients together. Add enough *Curry Dressing* (see page   ) to moisten.
    Serves 4

Coleslaw

1 *lb cabbage (approx.)*   1 *tart apple, cored, but not
                                        peeled*

1 *green or red pepper*
1 *carrot*
1 *teaspoon sea kelp*

2 *tablespoons mayonnaise*
1 *tablespoon lemon juice (or
   more, to taste)*

Shred or grate the cabbage, apple, pepper and carrot. Add kelp and mix well. Add mayonnaise and lemon juice and mix very well.

Serves 6

Lentil Salad

1 *cup lentils*
2 *cups water*
1 *bay leaf*
1 *garlic clove*
1 *small onion*

$\frac{1}{3}$ *cup minced parsley*
1 *medium, minced onion*
3 *tablespoons peanut oil*
2 *tablespoons cider vinegar*
1 *tablespoon lemon juice*

Heat water to boiling. Add small onion, bay leaf and garlic clove. Sprinkle in lentils and simmer covered 25–30 minutes or until lentils are just tender. Drain lentils, rinse with cold water to cool and remove onion, bay leaf, and garlic.

Heat the peanut oil in a small frying pan. Sauté minced onion until just transparent. Remove from heat and let cool.

Place lentils in large bowl, add sautéed onion, including oil. Mix well. Add parsley, vinegar and lemon juice. Toss.

Serves 4.

This is a very basic recipe to which you may add any of your favourite herbs, spices or raw vegetables. As lentils have a rather bland taste, they go well with many other foods.

Spinach and Yogurt Salad

1 *lb. fresh spinach*
½ *teaspoon fresh lemon juice*
1 *spring onion, minced*

1 *small container yogurt*
1 *tablespoon fresh mint (½*
   teaspoon dried)

Wash spinach and strip away stems. Save a few leaves for a garnish and chop the rest very finely. Mix the chopped spinach with the lemon juice, spring onion and yogurt. Chill at least 1 hour.

To serve, place the yogurt mixture on a bed of spinach leaves and garnish with mint.

Serves 4.

Soy Granule Salad
A variation on a Middle Eastern theme

½ *cup soy granules*
8 *fl. oz. water*
⅓ *cup lemon juice*
1 *cup chopped parsley, prefer-*
   able flat-leafed
1 *medium size onion, minced*
2 *large, ripe tomatoes, chopped*

1 *teaspoon salt*
⅓ *cup oil (at least 2 tablespoons*
   of which should be olive oil)
1 *cup chopped fresh mint or 1*
   tablespoon crumbled dried
   mint

Soak the soy granules in the water for 10 minutes. Line a sieve with cheesecloth and drain the granules, wrap the granules in the cloth and wring to remove as much water as possible. Toss the granules with the lemon juice and chill the mixture until ready to serve.

Just before serving, toss the granule-lemon juice mixture with the remaining ingredients.

Serves 4.

Sprout!

Seeds contain the germ of life. Sprout a seed and you have a living food which contains even *more* vitamins and minerals than the dormant seed. Sprouts are inexpensive, too. About ¼ cup of dry seed produces approximately two cups of sprouts. Sprouts can be grown almost any place, any time. With sprouts you can have fresh greens in the winter while your garden sleeps under a blanket of snow or in the heat of summer when leaves in the garden bolt and wilt faster than they can be picked. Sprouts come in a wide variety of flavours and textures as well. Cress produces fragile, peppery sprouts. Alfalfa sprouts are mild, delicious and delicate. Soybean sprouts are hearty and chewy. Bean sprouts are crisp and mild, while sprouted wheat is very sweet.

Almost any bean or seed can be sprouted. Sprouting material should be purchased at a natural food store, though, as garden seeds may have been chemically treated. Also, some varieties of beans and seeds have higher germination rates than others and are sold as "sprouting seeds." This is especially true of soybeans.

Sprouts may be grown in nearly anything as long as it isn't wooden. Metallic or lead-glazed pottery. A lid is essential. Sprouting material needs proper moisture, warmth and air circulation. The best temperature is between 75° and 85°F. Even if your home is kept cooler, you will probably be able to find a warm place such as under the kitchen sink or near the water heater, etc. Air circulation can be controlled by simply not crowding your sprouts. About one-third of your sprouting container should be used for air space. If you're planning on harvesting two cups of sprouts, use a container that will hold three cups. Moisture is easily maintained by rinsing the sprouts several times a day and keeping them properly drained. If you use a commercial sprouter that drains automatically, fine. If not, your sprouts should be rinsed in a colander or strainer and thoroughly drained before being returned to the sprouter. While rinsing and draining, remember that your sprouts are quite fragile and brittle, and treat them gently. Cool water is best.

Harvested sprouts should be well drained and refrigerated in airtight containers. They will keep about five days. If you'd like a little bonus of chlorophyll and attractive green leaves, you can cover your ready-to-harvest sprouts with a transparent lid or wrap and place them in the sun for several hours. Don't let them dry out. We like green leaves on alfalfa, cress and mustard sprouts, but the "greening" seems to make bean sprouts taste rather harsh. Try it anyway, it might be just to your taste.

To start, try sprouting beans, they are among the easiest to sprout. First, determine the amount of sprouts you'll want. Generally, one ounce of seeds will produce one cup of sprouts. Measure your beans. Soak the beans in water equal to four times the amount of beans. (One cup of beans requires four cups of water, for example.) Soak them overnight or about eight hours. Drain the beans in a colander, and save the water for watering your plants. Rinse the beans with cool water, drain them and place them in your sprouting container. Cover the container with a lid. If the container is transparent, put it in a dark place or cover it with a towel.

IMPORTANT: there should be *no* water accumulated in the bottom of the container. Now, if you rinse and drain your beans three times a day, you will have sprouts in three to five days. Each time you rinse, check for soft or "furry" beans and discard them. Sprouts are ready to be harvested when they taste good to you. Experimentation is your best guide. Some sprouts, such as wheat, fenugreek and sunflower are best when the sprout is about the same length as the seed. Bean sprouts should be about one and one half inches long, and we like alfalfa, mustard and cress when tiny leaves appear on the tip of the sprout.

Chia, cress and flax seeds are mucilaginous and sticky when soaked. We had a lot of trouble with them until we recalled the fresh cress sprouts we used to buy in the street markets of Amsterdam. They were sold in tiny, damp cardboard boxes in which they had been grown. We adapted the method by soaking our seeds as usual, then spreading white paper towels (two layers) in a perforated commercial sprouter. We poured the soaked seeds over the toweling, and covered the container as usual. Then, instead of rinsing and draining the seeds, we sprinkled them with water (a plant mister works beautifully) just enough to keep the towels damp but not wet. It worked. If you don't have a perforated sprouter, you might try screening, raised so that excess water can drain.

Soy bean sprouts can be difficult, but their high protein content makes them worth the trouble. Pick over your soybeans carefully before soaking them, and carefully remove any mushy or fuzzy beans as they sprout. We have raised soybeans in several different sprouters, and we've found that in all cases we're more successful if we rinse and drain the beans in a colander, then return them to the sprouter. If possible, rinse your soybeans about five times a day. Also, be sure to buy *sprouting* soybeans.

Sprouts may be used in cooked dishes, but are best eaten raw to preserve the precious vitamins, minerals and enzymes. Use sprouts generously in salads, sandwiches, dips and snacks. Lavishly garnish soups, cereals, cooked foods and desserts with sprouts. Sweet wheat sprouts are great for dessert. For some people, soybean sprouts are best used when lightly steamed or stir-fried, as they have a definite beany flavour. Still another way to reap the benefits of your harvest of sprouts is to whiz a handful in the blender with your favourite vegetable drink for a nutritious drink.

Sprouting is so easy and rewarding that it's a great pastime for kids. Sprouting can be very exciting, and they'll be eager to eat the sprouts they've grown. We've even had to pay for a long-distance call from a child who had forgotten to leave sprout-watering instructions during an overnight trip!

Another benefit of sprouting is the superior sandwich greens which can be made from sprouts. If you have to take a sandwich to school or the office, you *know* how limp your lettuce will be at lunchtime. Sprouts, on the other hand will stay crisp and crunchy for *hours* in a properly wrapped sandwich. Besides, the great variety of sprout flavours make sprouts more than an anonymous crunch — you can *flavour* your lunch with a lively, lovely sprout.

Sprouts are rich in many essential nutrients including assimilable minerals!

The Pursuit of Freshness

Gardens are a delight. There is nothing quite like the pleasure of being surrounded by a wealth of burgeoning herbs and vegetables. There are always plenty of things to be frozen and bottled and a wonderful variety of things from which to choose for daily meals. We often have four or five different vegetables for dinner or a spectacular casserole or salad with a myriad of herbs and vegetables.

As with any other food, freshness counts! The best place to eat vegetables might be in the garden, but that isn't usually practical. If you are picking your vegetables from the garden, though, it's best to eat them as soon after picking as possible. Our method is to take an early morning tour of the garden to see just what's available. By the time we're ready to cook dinner, we've narrowed the possibilities down to a few. Then we go and pick them just in time to cook. To ease chores, we often cook larger amounts than we need, and freeze the remainder for winter.

Gardens are where you find them. Patios, window-boxes, even flowerpots can provide a few favourite vegetables at their peak of freshness. One of our favourite and most prolific gardens is 18 stories in the air! Second best to having your own garden (or a generous neighbour) is to find a local farm shop. Try to get there just after it opens, as few of them have coolers, and you want your vegetables *fresh*. Bring your own cooler to transport your treasures.

Smaller local shops often buy from nearby farms. Local papers provide information as to what crops are abundant in your area. Not only will those be the freshest, they are most often the best bargains. Even large supermarkets sometimes buy local produce. If your supermarket has a special on something in season ask your produce manager if it is locally grown. You may be pleasantly surprised. Natural food stores often carry a good selection of local produce that is organically grown. Those natural food stores that do not carry fresh vegetables are often gold-mines of information on sources for farm-fresh vegetables. Many small farmers may not have enough extra produce to sell commercially, but *do* have a small surplus. Ask. You might be lucky enough to find a gardener who has planted more than he can use. Folks who are interested in organic gardening are usually interested in the whole natural foods movement, and may be regular customers at your natural food store.

Once you have found your fresh vegetables, treat them with the respect they deserve. Keep them chilled until you are ready to use them. Wash them very briefly with cool water, cook as short a time as possible, and *never* throw away the cooking water — it's full of vitamins and minerals. Use leftover cooking water for soups and stews.

It's not difficult in cooking vegetables to make them delightful taste-tempting treats if you cook them with kindness and respect.

1. Pick them just before cooking time or buy as fresh as possible and keep them chilled.

2. Wash *quickly* in cool water. Shake off excess water.

3. Steam in a covered pot with as little water as possible. A perforated steamer basket is helpful.

4. Save all cooking water. There are vitamins and minerals in it.

5. Cut vegetables in as little time as possible to conserve nutrients.

6. Use your eyes! When a vegetable changes colour, it's done. Stringbeans, for example, turn from light green to bright green. When they are overdone, they turn greyish-green.

7. Cooking times are always relative. Roots take longer to cook than stems. Stems take longer to cook than leaves. Don't toss everything into the pot at one time. Let each part be done to its intrinsic timetable. This is the single

most important rule in the cooking of vegetables. Learn it well and you won't need a cookbook. You won't even need to know the name of the vegetable. This is a great help when you find something so unfamiliar that you couldn't look it up in a cookbook, anyway.

You do not need to carry a chart of food values around with you in order to know what you are eating. Remember the rule about eating green and yellow vegetables every day? Well, generally, the deeper green or orange a vegetable is, the more vitamin value it has. This is graphically illustrated by such things as courgettes and cucumbers which have considerable Vitamin A as long as they are *unpeeled*. Remove the dark green skin and you have thrown away the Vitamin A. Red, ripe, sweet peppers have about four times the Vitamin C of oranges with about one-third less calories. Even the immature green peppers have more Vitamin C than oranges. Cooked green peppers have more Vitamin C than oranges. Cooked green peppers, for instance, have 96 mg. of Vitamin C per 100 grams, as compared to 50 mgs. average per 100 grams of raw oranges.

Since we depend on vegetables for the major part of our diet, we boost their protein value by adding high-protein foods to many recipes. Vegetables, on a rough average, have about one and one-half grams of protein per 100 grams. Natural cheese has about 25 grams of protein per 100 grams, and eggs have about 12.9 grams. We also like to use soy granules which are available in our health food store. Their protein content is about 50 percent and the taste and texture makes them compatible with a wide range of foods. We use them liberally.

Note: Avoid cucumbers with waxed skins. These skins must be removed, thus destroying virtually all of the Vitamin A!

Broccoli Mayonnaise Vert

2–4 cups broccoli florets

MAYONNAISE VERT

1 *teaspoon chopped chives*	1 *tablespoon lemon juice*
1 *tablespoon chopped parsley*	1 *tablespoon vinegar*
½ *teaspoon chopped tarragon or*	½ *teaspoon salt*
basil or oregano	1 *egg, lightly beaten*
½ *teaspoon liquid lecithin*	8 *fl. oz oil (at least ¼ should be*
	olive oil)

Cook the broccoli florets in boiling salted water until just tender-crisp. Drain. Rinse with cold water. Chill.

Place in a blender the chives, parsley, tarragon (or whatever), lecithin, lemon juice, vinegar, salt, egg and a quarter of the oil. Blend thoroughly. With the blender at low speed, trickle the remaining oil in a slow, steady stream until all the oil is absorbed and the mayonnaise is thick. Chill.

Toss the broccoli with a small amount of mayonnaise, just to coat. Serve with a dollop of mayonnaise to garnish.
Serves 4–6.

Spinach with Rice

½ *lb. fresh spinach*	2½ *cups water*
¼ *cup oil*	*salt and pepper to taste*
5 *spring onions, chopped*	1 *teaspoon dried oregano*
(green part, too.)	*grated Parmesan cheese*
½ *cup raw brown rice*	

Wash spinach carefully. Remove the stems and tear the spinach into approximately 1½ inch square pieces. Drain and set aside. Heat the oil and sauté the spring onions until soft. Add the rice and stir until the rice is well coated with oil. Add the water and bring to a boil. Cover and cook for about 25 minutes or until rice is done. Add salt, pepper and oregano. Taste for seasoning. Add the spinach. Cover the pot and let the spinach steam for 2 minutes. Stir the spinach into the rice and cook over low heat for 5 minutes more. Serve with a sprinkle of parmesan.

Serves 4.

Super Tomato-Vegetable Pie

Whole wheat pie crust for an open pie (see page 177)	*1 medium courgette, sliced*
3 teaspoons olive oil	*3 tablespoons chopped parsley*
2 large onions	*¼ teaspoon thyme*
1 clove garlic, crushed	*salt and pepper to taste*
6 large tomatoes, peeled and sliced	*2 eggs, beaten until frothy*
	2 oz. grated cheese (Cheddar is good)

Press dough into a pie plate and bake at 450°F. for 7 minutes. Remove from oven and turn heat to 400°F.

Heat the olive oil and sauté onions and garlic until onions are soft. Add tomatoes, courgette, parsley and thyme and simmer until courgette is barely soft. Add salt and pepper to taste. Place vegetable mixture into crust. Top with the eggs and sprinkle with the grated cheese. Bake for about 15 minutes or until lightly golden.

Vegetable Stroganoff
If you thought Stroganoff was a beef dish, this should be a delicious surprise.

2 cups cooked vegetables (use your imagination)	*1 cup rich stock or vegetable cooking water*
2 tablespoons vegetable oil	*1 teaspoon Dijon mustard*
1 tablespoon butter	*½ cup sautéed mushrooms (optional)*
1 large onion, sliced thinly	*1 small container plain yogurt*
3 tablespoons whole wheat flour	

Heat the vegetable oil and butter together until the butter

melts. Sauté the onion in the mixture until just transulcent. Add the flour and stir to mix well. Add the stock gradually, stirring, until the sauce thickens (about 5 minutes). Add the vegetables and mushrooms to the sauce. Remove from heat and stir in the yogurt.

Serve over hot cooked pasta.

Serves 4.

Courgettes El Greco

½ *onion, chopped*
4 *small courgettes, sliced*
1 *clove garlic, crushed*

2 *tablespoons olive oil*
½ *teaspoon dried oregano*
salt and pepper to taste

Put all ingredients into a small pot, bring to a boil, cover tightly, and simmer 7–10 minutes, or until the courgettes are just barely tender.

Serves 4.

Vegetables Vinaigrette

½ *cup carrots cut into finger-size pieces*
½ *cup celery cut in finger-size pieces*
½ *cup asparagus tips*
½ *cup spring onions, white part only, cut in 1½" lengths*

½ *cup small, fresh mushroom caps*
1 *cup Vinaigrette Sauce (see page 185)*

Cook the carrots, celery, asparagus and spring onions SEPARATELY in boiling, salted water, until just tender-crisp. Drain, rinse with cold water, drain again thoroughly.

Place all of the vegetables, including the mushroom caps, in a glass bowl. Add the vinaigrette sauce and toss to mix well. Cover and refrigerate for at least eight hours, tossing occasionally. To serve, drain and arrange on a platter. Serve cold or at room temperature.

Serves 4.

Scalloped Potatoes

6 *medium potatoes, sliced (not*
   peeled)
1 *green pepper, chopped finely*
2 *medium onions, sliced*
salt and pepper to taste

whole wheat flour
$\frac{3}{4}$ *pint milk, or* $\frac{3}{4}$ *pint stock with*
   $\frac{1}{2}$ *cup powdered milk*
oil or butter

Oil or butter a 4 pint casserole. Heat oven to 350°F.

Place a layer of potatoes in the bottom of the casserole, using about one third of the potatoes. Sprinkle with half of the peppers and half of the onions. Sprinkle with salt and pepper and a little flour. Add one third more potatoes and repeat the previous layer. Add the remaining potatoes. Add the milk or stock. Brush the top layer with oil or butter. Cover the casserole and bake at 350°F. for 45 minutes, uncover and cook 15 minutes more, or until lightly browned.

Vary by adding parsley, thyme or other herbs.
Serves 4.

Scalloped Potatoes with Ham

Add to the above recipe 2 cups chopped ham, and substitute ham broth for the stock if possible. Add the ham in the onion-pepper layer and proceed as above.

Mixed Vegetable and Cheese Casserole

2 *carrots*
1 *onion*
2 *turnips (about 1 lb.)*
2 *small potatoes (about $\frac{1}{2}$ lb.)*
$\frac{1}{4}$ *lb. mushrooms, sliced*
$\frac{1}{2}$ *cup chopped parsley*
$1\frac{1}{2}$ *oz whole wheat flour*

$1\frac{1}{2}$ *teaspoons salt*
$\frac{1}{4}$ *teaspoon each, thyme and*
   basil
4 *oz. mild cheddar cheese,*
   grated
$\frac{1}{2}$ *cup soy granules*
$1\frac{2}{3}$ *cup stock or water*

Slice the carrots, onion, turnips and potatoes. Oil a 5-pint casserole. Preheat oven to 350°F.

Arrange the vegetables in a layer about 2 slices deep. Sprinkle with about ⅓ each of the parsley, flour, salt, herbs, cheese and soy granules. Make another layer of vegetables, sprinkle as before with ⅓ of the remaining ingredients. Make a final layer of vegetables, top with the remaining ingredients and pour the stock over all. Cover and bake 50 minutes at 350°F., removing the cover during the last 15 minutes.

Serve hot.

Serves 4–6.

Swede Purée

1½ *lbs. swedes, diced**
½ *cup water*
1 *small onion, chopped*
3 *oz. mild, cheddar cheese, grated*

¼ *cup toasted wheat germ*
salt and pepper to taste

Place the swedes, water and onion in a heavy pot, bring to a boil, cover closely, lower the heat to barely simmering, and steam until the swede is tender. The amount of time will depend upon the age of the swedes. Drain and reserve the cooking liquid.

Mash the swede and onion, or force it through a food mill. Whip in the cheese, wheat germ, salt and pepper. If the purée is too thick, add some of the cooking liquid (or save it for soup.)

Serve hot.

Serves 4.

*Young, un-waxed, organically-grown swedes need not be peeled.

Tofu with Vegetables

1 *teaspoon vegetable oil*   ¼ *lb. mushrooms, sliced*

1 *carrot, sliced*
1 *small onion, sliced*
1 *cup fresh mung bean sprouts*
2 *cloves garlic, crushed*
½ *teaspoon salt*
1 *cake tofu, cut in cubes*

3 *tablespoons soy sauce*
2 *tablespoons sesame tahini*
½ *teaspoon honey*
1 *tablespoon tomato paste*
¼ *teaspoon freshly ground ginger*

Heat the oil in a wok or heavy frying pan. Add the mushrooms, carrots and onions. Stir vigorously for about 2 minutes. Add all of the remaining ingredients. Cover the pot and steam for 3 minutes. Serve hot.

Serves 2.

Favourite Tomatoes

1 *large tomato per serving*
1 *tablespoon blue cheese and* 1
   tablespoon wheat germ for
   each slice

Remove the stem ends from the tomatoes. Slice thickly, about three slices per tomato. Top each slice with one tablespoon blue cheese and on tablespoon wheat germ. Grill until the cheese is bubbly.

Courgette-Cheese Casserole

1 *lb, courgettes, diced*
¼ *pint water*
2 *eggs*

2 *oz. grated Cheddar cheese*
¼ *cup wheat germ*
salt to taste

Heat oven to 400°F. Oil a 3 pint casserole.

Place the courgettes and water in a heavy pot. Bring to a boil, cover, and simmer 5–7 minutes or until barely tender. Drain, reserving the water for soup or other cooking.

Beat the eggs and mix with the drained courgettes and

half of the cheese. Add salt to taste. Place the mixture into the prepared casserole. Sprinkle with the remaining cheese and top with the wheat germ.

Bake 25 minutes, or until hot and bubbly.
Serves 4.

Scalloped Tomatoes

1 *small onion, chopped*	1 *tablespoon minced parsley*
1 *small sweet green pepper, chopped*	*pinch thyme*
	$\frac{1}{2}$ *teaspoon salt*
4 *tablespoons oil*	4 *tablespoons wheat germ*
2 *cups whole wheat bread cubes*	6 *medium tomatoes, peeled and sliced*
1 *clove garlic, squished through a press*	

Heat oven to 350°F.

Cook onion and green pepper in one tablespoon oil until soft. Heat the remaining oil and toss the bread cubes in it until they begin to crisp. Add the garlic, parsley and thyme and mix well. Set aside.

Place half of the sliced tomatoes in an oiled, 3 pint casserole. Top with half of the salt, half of the bread cubes, half of the wheat germ and all of the onion mixture. Add the rest of the tomatoes, top with the remaining bread, salt, and wheat germ.

Bake 30 minutes.
Serves 6.

Savoury Pumpkin Ring

2 *cups pumpkin purée*	$\frac{3}{4}$ *cup fresh wholewheat bread crumbs*
2 *tablespoons oil*	
1 *small onion, chopped*	$\frac{1}{4}$ *cup wheatgerm*
1 *small stalk celery with leaves, chopped*	*dash allspice*
	$\frac{1}{2}$ *teaspoon salt*

2 *teaspoons honey*   2 *fl. oz. milk*
2 *eggs, beaten*

Put the pumpkin purée in a large bowl.

Oil a two-pint ring mould and pre-heat oven to 350°F.
Heat oil and sauté onion and celery until just translucent.
Add bread crumbs and sauté. Add sautéed mixture to
pumpkin and mix well. Stir in wheatgerm, allspice, salt
and honey. Mix eggs and milk together and add to the
pumpkin mixture. Pour purée into the ring mould. Set
mould in pan of hot water and bake about 45 minutes or
until set. Unmould onto warm plate.

This is very nice with a cooked green vegetable served
in the centre of the ring.

Serves 6.

Pumpkin Purée

Wash the pumpkins well, cut them open and remove the
seeds and pulp. Set the seeds and pulp aside. Cut the
pumpkin into chunks, about 2″. Put the chunks into a
heavy pan and add enough water to make about 2″ of
liquid. Cover the pan tightly. Bring the water to a boil,
lower the heat and steam the pumpkin for about 30
minutes or until very soft. Let it cool a little. Purée the
pumpkin through a food mill or in a blender.

Pumpkin purée may be seasoned and served as a
vegetable, or used in soups, or whatever you like.

Pumpkin Seeds

Separate the pumpkin seeds from the mushy pulp. Spread
the seeds in a single layer on a baking sheet and toast them
at 350°F., stirring once or twice, for about 10 minutes or
until lightly browned.

Garden Burgers

1 *carrot*
1 *small courgette*
1 *small onion*
3 *tablespoons soy granules*
2 *tablespoons wheat germ*
½ *teaspoon salt*

2 *tablespoons corn meal*
3 *eggs*
1 *tablespoon chopped parsley*
vegetable oil (about 2 tablespoons.)

Grate the carrot, courgette and onion together. Mix with the soy granules, wheat germ, salt and corn meal. Separate two of the eggs. Beat the yolks with the whole egg, and add to the vegetable mixture. Beat the two remaining whites stiff, but not dry. Add the parsley to the vegetable mixture. Gently fold in the eggwhites. Oil and heat a griddle or heavy frying pan. Drop vegetable mixture by teaspoonfuls onto the griddle. Cook slowly about 4 minutes on each side. To vary, add any chopped herb you fancy.

Makes about 18 burgers – 3 per serving.

Vegetable Spectacular
Worth the time it takes!

1 *courgette, sliced*
1 *yellow squash, sliced*
1 *cup broccoli florets*
½ *cup fresh green peas*
2 *carrots, peeled and cut into sticks*
1 *cup green beans, trimmed*

6 *small cabbage leaves, stem vein removed*
5 *medium potatoes (about 1½ lbs.) peeled and diced*
1½ *oz. soft butter*
salt and pepper to taste
2 *oz melted butter*

Each vegetable must be cooked *separately* in salted water until very slightly tender — not "done," because more cooking will follow. Cook courgette, squash, broccoli, peas, carrots, beans and cabbage, drain each vegetable and rinse with cold water. Keep separate. Boil potatoes in salted water until thoroughly cooked. Drain, and return potatoes to low heat to dry. Add salt and pepper and mash thoroughly.

Heat oven to 350°F. With the soft butter, thickly grease a 3 pint ovenproof bowl. Place a broccoli floret flower side down in the centre of the bowl and surround with a ring of overlapping courgette slices, then a ring of squash slices, then a row of carrot sticks and beans, filling the spaces with peas. Continue to make designs until the top of the bowl is reached. Pat a thin layer of mashed potatoes over your design. Sprinkle with salt and pepper. Add a layer of cabbage leaves. Fill the bowl with the remaining vegetables, ending with a layer of cabbage and a final layer of mashed potatoes. Add salt and pepper as you go. Pour the melted butter over the vegetables and bake at 350°F. for 30 minutes. Run a knife around the mould and unmould it carefully onto a serving plate. Serve immediately.

Serves 4–6.

Zesty Brussels Sprouts

1 *lb. Brussels sprouts*	$\frac{1}{2}$ *teaspoon caraway seeds*
2 *tablespoons water*	2 *tablespoons plain yogurt*
3 *tablespoons lemon juice*	1 *tablespoon grated onion*

Trim stems from sprouts and remove all tough and discoloured leaves. Steam the sprouts with the water, lemon juice and caraway seeds for about 12 minutes or until barely tender. Drain and reserve the liquid and keep the sprouts warm. Add the yogurt and onion to the reserved steaming liquid and mix thoroughly. Toss with the Brussels sprouts. Serve hot.

Serves 4.

Stuffed Acorn Squash

2 *acorn squash, halved and seeded*	4 *teaspoons honey*
	salt and pepper to taste
2 *oz. butter*	

Oil a baking dish large enough to hold the squash. Heat oven to 350°F. Prick the fleshy side of the squash with a fork, being careful not to pierce the skin. Place butter and honey in the cavity of each squash. Season to taste. Bake about 1 hour.

Serves 4.

Gratinée of Cauliflower

1 *large cauliflower*	2 *oz. freshly grated Parmesan*
2 *eggs*	*cheese*
½ *cup skimmed milk*	1 *oz. butter*
salt and pepper to taste	

Heat oven to 450°F.

Break cauliflower into florets and steam in a small amount of salted water until barely tender. Drain the cauliflower and mash it coarsely. Whisk together the eggs and milk and mix with the cauliflower. Season to taste. Place mixture in a baking dish which has been lightly buttered. (Individual casseroles are nice.) Sprinkle with the cheese and butter. Bake 20 minutes in 450°F. oven.

Note: Smaller baking dishes may cook more quickly.

Serves 4.

Potato Pancakes

½ *onion, grated*	3 *tablespoons chopped parsley*
1 *large potato, grated and rinsed (do not peel)*	1 *teaspoon lemon juice*
⅓ *cup water biscuit crumbs*	2 *tablespoons plain yogurt*
	oil

Mix together the onion, potato, crumbs, parsley, lemon juice and yogurt. Make 4 pancakes. Cook slowly in a little oil in a large frying pan over moderate heat until quite brown on both sides. Serve hot.

Serves 2.

Versatile & Nutritious Bean Curd

The Chinese are credited with "discovering" bean curd almost twenty centuries ago, and it has been a dietary staple ever since. If you speak Chinese, it is called *doufu*, (the Japanese word is *tofu*). *Doufu* simply means bean cake, so the English "bean curd" is really more descriptive. Bean curd is made by precipitating and coagulating a liquid preparation of soybeans, much in the way cheese is made from milk. Don't make the mistake of calling bean curd "bean cheese," though, as the Chinese make a fermented bean curd which is very pungent and is called bean cheese.

Bean curd can be made at home, but is becoming more widely available. Most stores carry little plastic tubs of *Lao Doufu*, firm bean curd, and water. These tubs, if unopened, keep several weeks in a refrigerator. Once opened, the bean curd should be rinsed with cold water, stored in the refrigerator and covered with fresh water which is changed daily. It will keep about five days. Bean curd can be frozen, but the texture becomes coarse and spongy.

Freshly made bean curd can be found in Chinese shops and is bought by the square (*koh*). It can be stored under water in the refrigerator for about a week. Some natural food stores carry fresh bean curd, most will have bean curd in some form.

Many people characterize bean curd as flavourless. Actually, it has a very subtle, fresh flavour. Once you have grown to love it, the flavour is one that you crave. Many Chinese writers and philosophers have told of their craving for bean curd above all the spicy, elaborate and costly dishes available. Longing for bean curd is often equated with home-sickness!

The plainness and simplicity of flavour make bean curd an excellent foil for a multitude of tastes. The texture can also be altered in a number of ways. Cubes of bean curd make an excellent addition to clear soups or salads. The cakes can be sliced, mashed, steamed, stewed, boiled, fried or baked. Real *aficionados* like it cold, with a dip of soy sauce or oyster sauce for a delightful snack. Lemon juice and minced spring onions is an alternative, low-sodium dip.

If the culinary versatility of bean curd makes it sound like a miracle food, the economic and nutritional qualities elevate it to the realm of the truly miraculous. One cake of bean curd, about 120 grams, contains the following: 9.4 grams protein, 5 grams of mostly polyunsaturated fat (no cholesterol), 2.9 grams of carbohydrate and these vitamins and minerals:

Calcium	154 mg.
Phosphorus	151 mg.
Iron	2.3 mg.
Sodium	8 mg.
Potassium	50mg.
Thiamin	.07 mg.
Riboflavin	.04 mg.
Niacin	.1 mg.

Other studies list the following values for 100 grams of bean curd: Magnesium 27 mg; Zinc 0.6 mg.; Cobalt 5 mcg; and traces of pyridoxine, pantothenic acid and folic acid. The calorific content of the 120 gram cake is only *84* calories!

Fresh bean curd is not expensive, making it a nutritional bargain well worth trying.

Curried Bean Curd
(No added salt)

1 tablespoon oil
14 oz. bean curd in ½" dice
1 large onion, diced
1 clove garlic, chopped
1 tablespoon curry powder
pinch each cayenne pepper and
   allspice powder
3 tomatoes, peeled, seeded and
   chopped
1½ oz. raisins

1 cup cooked cauliflower
   florets
juice of 1 lemon
1 teaspoon lemon peel
½ cup water
2 tablespoons dry sherry
1 teaspoon cornflour or arrowroot mixed with 2 teaspoons
   water

Heat the oil in a large frying pan and sauté the onion and garlic briefly. Do not allow the garlic to brown. Add the curry powder, cayenne and allspice and mix well. Stir in the tomatoes, raisins, cauliflower, lemon juice, lemon peel and water. Bring to a boil and cook, stirring until the tomatoes are soft. Stir in the sherry and bean curd. Return to a boil. Add the cornflour or arrowroot mixture while stirring gently. Serve hot.

Makes 2 main dish portions, 4 side dish portions.

Chow Doufu (Stir-fry Bean Curd)

1 teaspoon oil
2 cloves garlic, crushed
6 spring onions in 1" pieces
1 cup sliced mushrooms
2 cups celery cabbage, sliced
   thin
1 teaspoon grated fresh ginger
2 tablespoons soy sauce

½ cup stock or water
½ cup fresh or frozen peas
14 oz. bean curd in ½ dice
1 cup fresh bean sprouts
1 teaspoon cornflour or arrowroot mixed with 2 teaspoons
   water

Heat the oil in a wok or large frying pan. Add the garlic. When the garlic browns, discard it. Add the spring onion and mushrooms. Stir briskly. Stir in the cabbage. Mix well. Add the ginger, soy sauce and stock. Bring to a boil over high heat. Add the peas and bean curd. Allow to simmer, stirring for 2 minutes. Taste for seasoning. Stir in the sprouts and the cornflour or arrowroot mixture. Serve hot.

Makes 2 main dish portions, 4 side dish portions.

Bean Curd à L'Orange

For each portion: 2 slices bean curd about ½″ × 4″ × 4″
SoySauce

SAUCE MIXTURE

3 *tablespoons minced onion*
5 *tablespoons orange juice*
1 *teaspoon grated orange peel*
1 *tablespoon lemon juice*
¼ *teaspoon cinnamon powder*

¼ *cup red wine*
1 *teaspoon cornflour or arrow-*
   root mixed with 2 teaspoons
   water

Brush the bean curd slices generously with soy sauce. Place on an oiled rack and grill until nicely browned, turning to brown both sides and brushing with soy sauce as desired. Set aside and keep warm.

Mix the sauce ingredients and bring to a boil. Stir the cornflour or arrowroot mixture into the boiling liquid. Pour over the bean curd. Serve hot.

This is enough for 2 portions. The recipe may be doubled.

Beehive Bean Curd

14 *oz. bean curd*
cold water to cover

SAUCE

2 *tablespoons Chinese oyster*
   sauce
1 *teaspoon soy sauce*
¼ *cup chicken or vegetable stock*

½ *teaspoon honey*
1 *teaspoon cornflour or arrow-*
   root
2 *teaspoons Chinese sesame oil*

Place the bean curd in water to cover. Bring to a boil and cook over fairly high heat 30 minutes. Remove the curds with a slotted spoon and drain. Allow to cool. Slice each cooled cake into 9 pieces.

Mix together all the sauce ingredients. Bring to a boil in a large, shallow pan. Add the bean curd and simmer for about 10 minutes, covered tightly. Remove the cover and stir the bean curd gently until the sauce is absorbed.

Serve on a bed of steamed or stir-fried chinese leaves or spinach. Drizzle the sesame oil over for a garnish.

Serves 2 as a main dish, 4 as a side dish.

Basic Quick Aspic

1½ *pints vegetable stock or juice*
4 *envelopes gelatin (2 ounces)*
salt and pepper to taste
2 *egg shells, crushed*

2 *egg whites, lightly beaten*
2 *tablespoons vinegar, sherry or Cognac*

Mix the gelatin into the stock and let soften for 5 minutes. Heat the stock slowly to boiling to dissolve the gelatin. Season with salt and pepper to taste. Stir in the egg shells and whites. Boil 2 minutes. Remove from heat and stir in the vinegar or wine.

Dampen a linen tea towel with cold water and wring it out. Spread the towel in a colander and pour the stock through it. Chill the stock until it is about the consistency of raw egg white. Use the aspic to make a moulded salad or glaze. See Vegetable-Tofu Aspic. If aspic becomes too solid, heat it a little. To unmould aspic, dip the mould in warm water briefly and unmould onto a chilled plate.

Vegetable-Tofu Aspic

2½ *cups assorted raw or cooked vegetables*

2 *cups bean curd in ½ inch dice*
1 *recipe Basic Quick Aspic*

Chill a large bowl or decorative mould and pour in enough aspic to coat it by about ¼ inch. Arrange a layer of vegetables on the aspic, forming a design, if possible. Add enough aspic to coat the vegetables. Add a layer of bean curd. Add the remaining vegetables, bean curd and aspic and chill until set. Serve with salad dressing, mayonnaise or Lemon Soy Sauce.

Lemon Soy Sauce

juice of one lemon
good quality all-purpose soy
   sauce

Measure the lemon juice and add an equal quantity of soy sauce. Keep refrigerated. (It will last about a week.)

Lemon soy is good as a dressing for salads, a dip for bean curd or a condiment. Highly flavourful, it nevertheless dilutes the saltiness of the soy sauce. In Japanese cuisine, it is often served in small individual bowls as an at-the-table seasoning dip.

Vegetable-Bean Curd Balls with Sicilian Sauce
Marco Polo never had it so good!

14 *oz. bean curd*
2 *large eggs*
3 *tablespoons arrowroot*
1 *teaspoon oil*
2 *tablespoons minced onion*
1 *cup cooked, chopped mushrooms*
½ *cup cooked carrot, finely chopped*

2 *tablespoons soy sauce*
1 *cup whole wheat bread crumbs*
1 *teaspoon salt*
3 *tablespoons chopped fresh parsley*

Mash the bean curd and squeeze out as much liquid as possible. Drain. Place the drained curd in a large bowl.

Beat the eggs lightly and mix with bean curd. Sprinkle the arrowroot over and mix well. Heat the oil and sauté the onion, mushrooms and carrot together until the onion is soft. Stir in the soy sauce. Remove from heat and stir in the bread crumbs, salt and parsley. Stir the mixture into the bean curd. Mix very well. Form the mixture into balls about 1½″ around. Place the balls on an oiled pan and grill until lightly browned, turning to brown all sides. Simmer with Sauce Siciliana for 10 minutes, and serve hot.

Makes about 18 balls.

Sauce Siciliana

1 *small onion, finely diced*	½ *teaspoon dried oregano*
4 *cloves garlic, chopped finely*	1 *teaspoon dried basil*
2 *cups tinned tomatoes (chopped) with their juice*	*pinch fennel seed*
	½ *cup red wine*

Simmer all ingredients 20 minutes.

Makes about 2 cups.

Beans, Nuts & Seeds

Nuts are a delicious and nutritious food, high in protein, B vitamins, phosphorous, iron and calcium. They are also high in poly-unsaturated fatty acids, and when shelled are very prone to rancidity. Yet in most supermarkets, shelled nuts are not refrigerated, but are hung in little plastic bags on a rack. Nuts in the shell are gassed so that they will crack more neatly. They are bleached to uniformity of colour, and dyed for more eye appeal. Red dye does nothing whatever for the taste of pistachio nuts!

Many health food stores carry whole nuts in their natural state, and some even carry raw, shelled nuts. Shelled nuts, of course, must be kept under refrigeration. If you like toasted nuts, it is easy to toast your own, and there is nothing like the flavour of a freshly toasted nut! The effort of shelling your own nuts is a small price to pay for safe, wholesome food.

Seeds have many of the same nutritional qualities as nuts, although they are somewhat lower in fats, and therefore not as high in calories. Both seeds and nuts are rich foods; too rich to be a major protein source, but a delicious and valuable addition to any diet.

Simple foods are often the best, and freshly toasted nuts are no exception. They are also very simple to make. A cup or two of freshly shelled nuts are stirred in a heavy frying pan over moderate heat for about 10 minutes, or until they begin to smell delicious. Be careful not to scorch them! They may be sprinkled with a little salt while still hot, if you like. Try a combination of walnuts, almonds, cashews and pecans. Sprinkle a few chopped nuts on a favourite sandwich spread. Add chopped nuts to yogurt, or toss a few into rice or bulghur just before serving.

Beans are magic, as any child will tell you. A single bean might produce a sky-high stalk leading to an eventual pot of gold. More realistically, beans have been a staple in man's diet for thousands of years, often providing sustenance when no other food was available. Dried beans are portable, store well and multiply prolifically. They are a good source of protein when they are combined with those foods which allow all of the available amino acids to be utilized.

There are eight essential amino acids which are not synthesized in the human body, and must be obtained from the foods we eat. Unfortunately, these eight amino acids are usable only to the degree that they are balanced. That is, if one of the amino acids is deficient in a food, the other seven will be unusable in direct proportion to the deficiency. The balance is intrinsic in meats, seafood, eggs and dairy products. Among the pulses, soybeans have the most complete balance, but they are deficient in the sulphur-containing amino acids, while other pulses share that deficiency as well as lacking tryptophan. Fortunately, combining the pulses with other foods will compensate by matching strengths to deficiencies. Whole grains, seeds, nuts and milk may be used to complement the protein in beans.

Beans make a hearty and satisfying main dish, or a side dish that can accompany almost anything. We are fond of beans served with scrambled eggs for breakfast. Cooked beans may be marinated in French dressing and added to salads or simply eaten as a cold dish. Leftover beans may be added to soups, stews and casseroles. Try cold leftover beans with chopped onions and a dollop of yogurt. Beans are easy to cook, too, as the following instructions will show. Just keep in mind that beans cooked *slowly* tend to be less gas-producing.

To Cook a Bean

Method I: Soak beans overnight in water to cover by about 2 inches. The next day, add enough water to cover by about one inch and cook the beans at simmer for about an hour, or until the beans are soft.

Method II: Add enough water to cover the beans by about two inches. Heat to boiling and retain at a boil for two minutes. Remove from the heat and let soak for at least one hour. Add enough water to cover by about one inch, and simmer for about an hour or until beans are soft.

Both methods: Add additional water as needed. *Never* add salt until the beans are done, or you risk hard beans that no amount of cooking will soften.

Whenever possible, cook the beans a day ahead. Nearly all bean dishes are improved by waiting for a day or two.

Cooking Soybeans

1. Soak the soybeans 6 hours or overnight. ⅓ cup dry = 1 cup soaked.
2. Freeze the beans in soaking water, then cook for about 1 hour.

OR

Cook the soaked soybeans in a pressure cooker at 15 lbs. (standard) pressure for 45 minutes.

OR

Cook the soaked soybeans over low heat for several hours. Skim foam from the beans when they reach a boil.

Soy Snacks

Soak soybeans overnight in salted water. Boil one hour. Heat oven to 350°F. Spread the beans on a baking sheet to form a single layer. Bake 30 minutes, stirring every 10 minutes or so. If desired, add salt or seasoning while hot. Store in a tightly covered jar.

Festive Walnut Ring with Mushroom Sauce

1¼ *cups finely chopped celery*
¼ *cup minced onion*
1½ *cups wholewheat bread crumbs*

6 *oz. ground walnuts*
2 *tablespoons minced parsley*
1 *teaspoon herb salt or vegetable salt*

½ *teaspoon kelp*   ¼ *cup water*
¾ *pt. plain yogurt*   2 *tablespoons soy sauce*
3 *eggs lightly beaten*   2 *tablespoons oil*

Oil a 3 pint ring mould. Heat oven to 375°F.

In a large bowl, mix together the celery, onion, bread crumbs, walnuts, parsley, salt and kelp. Mix the yogurt mixture with the dry ingredients and mix well. Let stand 10 minutes. Smooth the mixture into the prepared mould and bake 45 to 50 minutes or until top is brown and side pulls away slightly from side of mould. Unmould onto a warm plate. Fill the centre of the ring with *mushroom sauce* (see page 189). Serve with extra sauce. Sprinkle with parsley.

Steamed Soy Sprouts

¼ *cup water*
dash salt
2 *cups soy sprouts*

Add the salt to the water and heat to boiling. Add the sprouts and cover. Steam for 4 minutes over moderate heat. Serve hot as a buttered vegetable, or add to cooked dishes, or chill and add to salads.

Fancy Beans

1½ *lbs. dwarf french beans,*   1 *teaspoon salt*
     sliced   1 *clove garlic, squished*
½ *cup water*

DRESSING
1 *tablespoon oil*   1 *tablespoon sesame seeds*
½ *teaspoon kelp powder*   2 *tablespoons soy granules or*
3 *oz. raw cashews, coarsely*   *powdered soy*
     chopped

Place the beans, water, salt and garlic in a heavy pot, bring to a boil over high heat. Cover, lower the heat to simmer and let cook 5 to 7 minutes, depending on the age and size of the beans. They should be tender-crisp and bright green.

While the beans cook, heat the oil and stir in the kelp, cashews and sesame seeds. Stir until the cashews and seeds are partially toasted. Stir in the soy granules and heat well. Toss the cooked beans with the dressing. Serve hot.

Serves 4.

Yankee Baked Soybeans
Worth the time it takes!

1 *cup dried haricot beans*	1 *teaspoon salt*
1 *cup dried soybeans*	$\frac{1}{2}$ *tea cup dark molasses*
$\frac{1}{4}$ *lb. lean salt pork,* without	$\frac{1}{4}$ *teacup honey*
nitrates (optional)	$\frac{1}{2}$ *teaspoon dry mustard*
1 *medium onion*	

Cover beans with water, bring to a boil and simmer 2 minutes. Cover and let stand 1 hour. Cook until tender (about an hour.) Add liquid as needed. Drain liquid from cooked beans and reserve it.

Put the beans in a large, heavy pot. (We prefer to conserve a bit of energy by using an electric slow cooker – but if you're baking, preheat the oven to 300°F.)

Score the pork into $\frac{1}{2}$ inch cubes, but do not cut through the rind. Cut the onion in chunks. Bury the onion in the beans, and push the salt pork into the beans so that only the rind is showing. Mix the remaining ingredients with the reserved bean liquid and pour over the beans. Cover the pot and cook slowly at 300°F. for 6–8 hours. Add boiling water as needed.

Serves 6.

Lentils and Rice Spanish Style

¼ *lb. lentils*
¼ *lb. brown rice*
1 *medium onion*
1 *large red pepper (as red as possible)*
1 *tablespoon olive oil*

1 *tablespoon peanut oil*
2 *peeled, seeded and chopped tomatoes*
1 *clove crushed garlic*
salt to taste

Cook lentils in 12 fl. ozs water with ½ teaspoon salt. Simmer uncovered about 30 minutes or until just tender.

Cook rice in 12 fl. ozs water with ½ teaspoon salt. Simmer uncovered about 35 minutes or until fluffy.

Chop onion and pepper into fairly small dice. Heat olive and peanut oil and sauté onions and pepper until they are a little soft. Add the tomatoes and garlic. Stir to mix well. Add rice and lentils and stir until everything is very well mixed.

There shouldn't be any liquid in the pan. If there is, just stir everything over gentle heat until it is all absorbed. Taste for seasoning.

Serves 6.

Lentil Loaf

12 *oz. lentils*
1 *teaspoon salt*
2 *tablespoons peanut oil*
1 *medium onion, minced*
1½ *oz. wheat germ*

1 *clove crushed garlic*
3 *tablespoons soy sauce*
2 *medium, peeled, seeded and chopped tomatoes*
2 *eggs, beaten*

Cook lentils in 2 pints water with the salt for about 35 minutes or until done. You need three cups of cooked lentils for this recipe so you will probably have some left over.

Heat oven to 350°F.

Heat peanut oil and sauté onion until transparent. Add onion and oil to three cups of cooked lentils. Add everything else. Oil loaf pan (mine is $8\frac{1}{2}'' \times 4\frac{1}{2}'' \times 2\frac{1}{2}''$, but if you wish to use smaller or larger ones, just watch cooking time). Add lentil mixture to the loaf pan, pat with fork to shape well and bake about 45 minutes.

This loaf is good hot or cold.

Serves 6.

Bean Pot

1 *lb. navy or haricot beans*
$2\frac{1}{2}$ *pints water*
8 *fl. oz. bean liquid*
$\frac{1}{2}$ *teacup molasses*

2 *teaspoons dry mustard*
$\frac{1}{2}$ *cup honey*
1 *large onion, chopped*

Soak the beans in the water for at least 6 hours. Cook the beans in the water for 2 to 3 hours, or until tender. Drain the beans, reserve the liquid.

Cook the beans, again, with 8 fl. oz. of the reserved liquid (use the rest for stock) and all of the remaining ingredients at very low heat in an oven or slow cooker for 10 to 12 hours.

Serves 6.

Lentil-Potato Casserole

4–5 *oz. lentils*
$\frac{3}{4}$ *pint water*
4 *medium unpeeled potatoes*
1 *small pepper, as red as possible*
2 *tablespoons peanut oil, or butter*
1 *oz. wholewheat flour*

8 *fl. oz water from cooking potatoes*
4 *fl. oz. cold water*
$\frac{1}{2}$ *cup instant type powdered milk*
1 *tablespoon salt*
$\frac{1}{4}$ *teaspoon thyme*
$\frac{1}{8}$ *teaspoon pepper*

Simmer lentils in water for about 40 minutes or until tender but not mushy. Drain. Reserve liquid.

Dice potatoes and cook in cold water to cover about 20

minutes or until tender. Drain potatoes. Save cooking water.

Heat oven to 375°F.

Dice pepper and onion.

Oil 4-pint casserole. Mix potatoes with lentils and place mixture in casserole.

Heat oil or butter in a frying pan, add onion and pepper and sauté briefly until just tender. Add flour, mix well and stir over very low heat 3 to 4 minutes to cook flour. Stir in 8 fl. oz of the potato water. (Save the rest of the potato and lentil liquid for soups.) Mix cold water with powdered milk and stir into flour mixture. Add salt, pepper and thyme. Cook, stirring, until mixture is slightly thickened. Pour hot sauce over potatoes and lentils, pop into oven and bake about 30 minutes or until top is browned and bubbly.

Serves 6.

Granule-Rice Croquettes

½ cup soy granules
1 cup cooked brown rice
1 tablespoon finely chopped chives or spring onion
¼ teaspoon dried thyme

2 eggs lightly beaten
¼ cup yogurt
4 fl. oz. tomato juice
oil

Mix together everything except the oil. Form into croquettes, cylinders or patties. Sauté in oil over medium heat until crisp and lightly browned on all sides.

Serve with tomato or white sauce.

Makes about 8 croquettes – 2 or 3 per serving.

Soy Pizza Crust

⅓ cup lukewarm water
½ oz. active dry yeast
pinch powdered ginger

4 oz. whole wheat flour
1½ oz. soy flour
1 tablespoon brewers' yeast

Add the active dry yeast and ginger to the water, cover and set in a warm place for about five minutes or until the yeast is becoming frothy. Stir in the remaining ingredients. Knead. Spread the dough on an oiled pizza pan or baking sheet by pressing the dough gently outwards from the centre. Cover and let rest in a warm place (75°F.) for about 10 minutes.

Heat oven to 450°F.

Topping
Sprinkle the pizza dough with the following ingredients, in order:

1½ cups *Pizza Sauce*
1 *teaspoon dried oregano*
½ *cup soy granules*
2 oz. *sliced mushrooms, lightly sautéed*

2 oz. *freshly grated Parmesan cheese*
2 oz. *freshly grated Mozzarella cheese*

Bake on the oven floor for about 10 minutes or until the cheeses are melted and bubbling.

Any of your favourite pizza ingredients may be added *between* the granules and the cheeses.

Super Granola

2 *cups rolled oats*
2 *cups rolled wheat*
½ *cup raw coconut*
½ *cup sesame seeds*
½ *cup wheat germ*
½ *cup date sugar*
½ *cup toasted peanut flour (optional)*

⅓ *cup cashews, chopped*
⅓ *cup walnuts, chopped*
⅓ *cup almonds, chopped*
⅓ *cup sunflower seeds*
2 *cups raisins, chopped*
½ *cup non-instant powdered milk*

Mix everything together. Store in a tightly covered jar, preferably in the refrigerator. Serve with milk.

Vary the ingredients as you like.

Soybean Rissoles

6 *oz. dry soybeans*
1 *tablespoon chopped parsley*
1 *small onion, chopped finely*
1 *oz. wheat germ*
3 *oz. whole wheat flour*
2 *fl. oz. soy sauce*
1 *teaspoon salt*

½ *teaspoon thyme*
½ *teaspoon basil*
½ *teaspoon celery seed*
¼ *cup cooking water from the beans (or stock or water)*
vegetable oil

Cook the beans. Drain them, reserving the liquid. Mash or chop the beans and mix in all the remaining ingredients except the oil.

Heat heavy frying pan, and cover the bottom with a small amount of vegetable oil. Form patties of the bean mixture and cook them over very low heat until crispy and brown, turning them once. The patties will be rather fragile and crumbly to start, but just handle them gently, they become more cohesive as they cook.

Makes about 8 rissoles.

Meatless Chili

1 *cup dried soybeans*
1 *cup lentils*
½ *cup sesame seeds*
2 *green or red peppers*
3 *medium onions*

2 *tablespoons peanut oil*
1 *tablespoon salt*
2 *tablespoons chili powder*
2 *cloves crushed garlic*
½ *teaspoon powdered cumin*

Wash soybeans and cover with cold water. Bring to a boil, remove from heat and let stand one hour. Drain beans, cover with fresh, cold water, bring to a boil and simmer over low heat one hour. Drain. Reserve liquid.

Place the lentils and sesame seeds in a large pot with water to cover, including the liquid from the soybeans. Bring to a simmer.

Chop peppers and onions finely. Heat peanut oil and sauté them briefly, until barely limp. Add them with oil to lentils. Add soybeans, salt, chili powder, garlic and cumin. Let simmer for about 30 minutes, or until everything is tender. Add more water if needed.

You might serve this with brown rice and a garnish of chopped raw onion, grated cheese, diced tomato, mashed avocado mixed with lemon juice or anything that strikes your fancy.

Serves 6 generously.

Soy-Vegetable Casserole

6 *oz. dry soybeans*
2 *stalks celery, diced*
2 *carrots, diced*
1 *medium onion, diced*
1 *swede, diced*
1 *green pepper, diced*
2 *teaspoons basil*
3 *tablespoons parsley*

2 *oz. whole wheat flour*
1 *tablespoon salt*
dash pepper
1 *cup hot stock, bean-cooking water, or water*
1 *tablespoon molasses*
juice of one lemon
wheat germ

Cook the soybeans. (See page 86).

Preheat the oven to 350°F. Oil a 2½ pint casserole.

Mix the cooked beans with the celery, carrots, onion, turnip, pepper, basil and parsley. Mix the flour with the salt and pepper, and toss the flour mixture with the bean-vegetable mixture. Place the mixture into the casserole. Mix the stock with the molasses and lemon juice, and pour the mixture over the contents of the casserole.

Bake covered for 30 minutes. Uncover. Sprinkle the top with wheat germ, and bake another 15–20 minutes or until the top is brown and bubbly.

Serves 4.

Calico Lentil Pot
A little of everything!

2 *tablespoons vegetable oil*   1 *large onion, chopped*

1 *leafy stalk celery, chopped*	$\frac{1}{2}$ *cup bulghur*
1 *pepper, chopped*	$\frac{1}{2}$ *teaspoon marjoram*
2 *cloves garlic, chopped*	$\frac{1}{4}$ *teaspoon thyme*
1 *cup tinned tomatoes*	2 *pints stock or water*
1 *cup lentils*	2 *teaspoons salt*
$\frac{1}{2}$ *cup brown rice*	

Put everything except the salt into a pressure cooker. (The cooker should never be more than $\frac{2}{3}$ full.) Heat, cover, seal and cook at 15 lbs. pressure (standard) for 10 minutes. Add the salt before serving.

This dish may, of course, be cooked in an ordinary saucepan. The cooking time would be about 45 minutes.

Toasting Sesame Seeds

Use a well-tempered, cast-iron frying pan. Layer the bottom with sesame seeds. Toast over moderate flame, stirring, until the seeds begin to brown and jump about in the pan. Remove the seeds immediately from the pan.

Aurora's Beans
Proving again that great dishes are often very simple

1 *lb. dried black-eyed peas, cooked*	4 *cloves garlic, chopped*
1 *teaspoon coarse sea salt*	1 *onion (preferably sweet) chopped very finely*
1 *teaspoon oregano*	

Place the salt, oregano, and garlic in a mortar, and grind with a pestle to a paste. Add the paste to the cooked beans and return the beans to a simmer. Cook, stirring occasionally, for 10 minutes or so, until the seasonings are well blended and most of the cooking liquid has been absorbed.

Serve hot, with a sprinkling of chopped onion.
Serves 4.

Chili Bean Loaf

3 *cups cooked navy or haricot*
  beans
1 *small green pepper, minced*
1 *small onion, minced*
1 *tablespoon oil*
1½ *cups fine, dry whole wheat*
  bread crumbs
2 *cloves garlic, squished*
  through a press

6 *oz. grated sharp cheese*
1 *tablespoon chili powder (or*
  more, if you like)
1 *teaspoon salt*
¼ *teaspoon basil*
½ *teaspoon cumin powder*
¼ *teaspoon celery seed*

Heat oven to 350°F. Oil a loaf pan or casserole.

Mix all ingredients thoroughly, and press the mixture lightly into the prepared pan.

Bake at 350°F. for one hour or until browned nicely. Serve hot or cold.

Soy Loaf

1 *stalk celery, grated*
1 *carrot, grated*
1 *onion, grated*
2 *tablespoons oil*
1 *oz. raw wheat germ*
2 *tablespoons soy sauce*

½ *teaspoon salt*
2 *eggs*
2 *cups cooked soybeans*
1 *tablespoon molasses or black*
  treacle
4 *fl. oz. tomato juice*

Pre-heat oven to 425°F.

Sauté the celery, carrot and onion in the oil for about five minutes or until the vegetables are quite limp. Add the wheat germ and continue sautéing for about one minute more. Beat together the soy sauce, salt and eggs. Mash the soybeans with the molasses and tomato juice. (The beans, molasses and juice may also be whirred in a blender if you prefer). Mix the vegetable mixture, egg mixture and the bean mixture together. Place in an oiled loaf pan. Bake at 425°F. for 30 to 40 minutes or until lightly browned.

Cheese

Cheese. What a wealth of images are contained in that word! Sharp, bright Cheddar; smooth, sophisticated Gruyere; bland Ricotta; rare and creamy Brie; rich, aristocratic Stilton; Roquefort, Parmesan, Gouda, Mozzarella, Feta, Bel Paese, Camembert. Once, not so long ago, the corner grocer sold only Cheddar, commonly known as "mouse-trap". Now the dairy case has slices of bright orange rubbery stuff which does have *some* cheese in it along with a number of other more dubious ingredients. What an indignity for an old friend! Cheese is thought to be as old as the domestication of animals — about *eleven thousand years*. Since then, cheese has developed in a variety of flavours and textures.

Cheese is alive. Throughout its life, various bacteria are playing out their roles in developing the cheese. Milk from virtually any animal may be used for cheese, although if it has been pasteurized, a starter must be added to produce the bacterial action which changes milk to cheese. Some cheeses have rennet added to promote coagulation. The coagulation of the milk produces curds (solid) and whey (liquid). The mass of curd is cut to whatever size is called for by a particular cheese. The curds might be heated in the whey before the whey is removed. The curds may be drained, torn, pressed, salted or whatever. For cheeses with mould, such as Stilton, Gorgonzola, Roquefort, etc., a mould-producing bacteria is added. The cheese may be eaten fresh or aged. During the aging process, new bacteria may make further changes in the cheese. In addition to all of the above, such flavourings as caraway seeds, pepper, sage and wine are used in some cheeses. The quality of cheese depends upon many of the factors surrounding its making. The freshness of the milk, its butter-fat content and the cow's diet have their effect on cheese. Cheeses are very pale in winter and bright yellow in summer. One can almost see the moment when summer grasses become more plentiful than winter hay. The time, temperature and humidity at which the cheese is stored will also affect the kind of cheese that results. Using cow's milk, a starter, salt and rennet, we have made "store cheese," Cheddar, Coullommiers, cream, cottage, a Greek country cheese (brined and unbrined), Scamorze and Riccotta. (We also make a blue which requires an additional bacteria for the blue mould.) Small differences in time, temperature and handling, produce vastly different cheeses.

Cheese needs little or nothing to enhance it as a food. It has high quality protein as well as calcium, phosphorus, vitamins and minerals. Cottage, quark, pot and Riccotta cheeses are relatively low in calories. Aside from all that, cheese is delicious. It can be eaten all alone or with fruit, dark bread or biscuits. It is usually best eaten at room temperature, but any cheese which is not being eaten should be kept cool. A whole cheese may look splendid on a buffet table or snack tray, but any left uneaten must be re-refrigerated, then brought to room temperature again at the next repast, resulting in an eventual loss of quality. Store cheese tightly wrapped to preserve moisture and at about 40°F. If your pantry is cool, refrigeration isn't necessary. Should mould develop on firm cheeses, it may be trimmed away.

It doesn't seem right to speak of cooking with cheese, as it's never really "raw." Using cheese in cooked foods is a matter of melting the cheese in order to combine it with other ingredients. At high temperatures, cheese gets tough and stringy. If you are grilling cheese, as for sandwiches, the grilling should be done quickly and only until the cheese melts. In most dishes using firm cheese and sauces, grated cheese may be added to a hot liquid or added to cool ingredients and cooked slowly at fairly low temperatures.

Some of the world's most magnificent cheeses come from this country, France, and Italy. The French seem to treat their cheeses with great reverence, while we are perhaps just a shade too matter-of-fact. No one, though has the humour and inventiveness of the Italians when it comes to cooking with cheese. Italy is justly proud of that greatest of seasoning cheeses, Parmesan, which is a fine flavouring ingredient, as well as the familiar "sprinkling" cheese with pasta. Unfortunately, Parmesan's popularity has led to a proliferation of a very inferior product, already grated and packaged in plastic shakers. Compared to freshly grated real Parmesan, it's pretty dull. However, it is rather like pepper — either you *always* grind it freshly, or you just don't care. Real Parmesan may be hard to find, but it is worth the search. Riccotta is an unusual cheese. It is made by adding skim milk to the whey left over from making cheese! It is creamy, low in calories and very mild in flavour, making it an excellent ingredient in many dishes.

Blinis

CRÊPES:

6 *eggs*	$\frac{1}{4}$ *teaspoon salt*
2 *fl. oz. water*	4 *tablespoons oil*
6 *oz. whole wheat flour*	

FILLING

1 *lb. dry cottage cheese, drain if necessary*	$\frac{1}{2}$ *teaspoon vanilla*
3 *tablespoons yogurt*	4 *tablespoons lecithin powder*
1 *egg yolk*	*oil for cooking*
2 *tablespoons honey*	

Beat the eggs and add the water. Add the flour a little at a time, mixing smooth. Beat in the salt and oil. The batter should be the consistency of heavy cream. Add water if you need to. Keep cool.

Mix all the filling ingredients together and keep chilled until needed.

Crêpes should be made in a crêpe pan or a frying pan with a bottom surface measuring about 7″–8″ in diameter. The pan should be oiled by rubbing it with a lightly oiled cloth, repeating as needed.

Heat the oiled pan over medium heat. Holding the pan with your left hand, drop a small ladleful of batter into the centre of the pan and quickly tip the pan to cover the entire bottom with batter. Let cook until the edges appear dry and delicately browned. Stack the crêpes on a plate, cooked side up.

Place a tablespoonful or two of the filling in the centre of the uncooked side of each crêpe. Fold two opposite sides of the crêpe towards the centre. Then, starting from a free end, roll the crêpe to cover the filling.

In an oiled pan, cook the rolled crêpes on both sides until delicately browned. Turn them very carefully, as they are prone to unfold rather easily.

Serve hot, topped with yogurt, sour cream, fruit, or whatever.

Serves 6–8.

Triple Cheese Bake

4 oz. cottage cheese
2 small courgettes, sliced thinly
3 fl. oz. tomato sauce

2 oz. grated Mozzarella or Scamorze
½ oz. freshly grated Parmesan

Oil a 2 pint casserole. Heat oven to 350°F. Put the cottage cheese in the casserole and top with a layer of half the courgettes. Sprinkle half the Mozzarella and half the tomato sauce over the courgettes. Repeat the courgettes, Mozzarella, tomato sauce layer. Top with the Parmesan. Bake one hour at 350°F.

Serves two as a main dish, four as a side dish.

French Toasted Cheese Sandwiches

2 *slices whole wheat bread* $\frac{1}{4}$ *teaspoon salt*
8 *slices cheddar or Swiss cheese*   *dash nutmeg*
2 *eggs*   *butter or oil*
6 *fl. oz. milk*

Make 4 sandwiches using two slices of cheese between each two slices of bread. Beat the eggs with the milk, salt and nutmeg. Dip the sandwiches in the egg mixture. Heat the butter or oil, and fry the sandwiches over moderate heat until they are golden brown and cheese is melted. Serve hot.
   Serves 4.

Golden Buck Rarebit

$\frac{1}{2}$ *oz. butter*   *salt and pepper to taste*
$\frac{1}{4}$ *lb. grated mild cheddar* $\frac{1}{4}$ *teaspoon dry mustard*
   cheese   2 *slices hot whole wheat toast*
3 *tablespoons milk*   2 *poached eggs*

Melt the butter over hot water in the top of a double boiler. Add the cheese and stir until melted. Stir in the milk. Season with the salt, pepper and mustard. Pour the hot cheese mixture over the toast and top each with a poached egg.
   Serves 2.

Cheddar-Walnut Pie

1 9-*inch pastry case, unbaked*   2 *eggs, lightly beaten*
1$\frac{1}{2}$ *cups whole wheat bread,* $\frac{1}{2}$ *teaspoon prepared mustard*
   crumbled   1 *cup grated Cheddar cheese*
6 *fl. oz boiling milk* $\frac{1}{2}$ *cup chopped walnuts*

Heat oven to 425°F. Put parchment over pie pastry, and

fill with dried beans. Bake in the hot oven for 15 minutes. Remove from the oven and remove the beans and parchment. Lower the oven temperature to 375°F.

Put bread in large bowl, pour boiling milk over it and let stand 5 minutes. Stir mustard into eggs, then mix eggs into bread mixture, stirring well. Stir in cheese and nuts. Pour into pie shell.

Bake at 375°F. for 30–35 minutes, or until the filling is set.

Serves 6.

NOTE: If the cheese you use is bland, you might want to add a pinch of salt. The recipe may be varied by adding finely chopped onion.

Baked Omelet

2 *tablespoons soy oil*
1 *small onion, minced*
4 *eggs, lightly beaten*
1 *oz. grated sharp Cheddar cheese*

2 *tablespoons plain yogurt*
kelp and pepper to taste
1 *tomato, peeled and sliced*

Heat oven to 425°F.

Heat the oil in an oven-proof dish or frying pan and sauté the onions until soft. Mix the eggs with the cheese, yogurt, salt and pepper and pour the mixture over the onions. Top with the tomato slices. Bake 10–15 minutes or until the eggs are set. Serve immediately.

Serves 2.

Cheese Spread

4 *oz. sharp Cheddar cheese, grated*
2 *oz. Neufchatel cheese at room temperature*

1 *teaspoon Dijon mustard*
½ *teaspoon garlic powder*
½ *teaspoon sweet paprika*
dash cayenne

Mash or mix in food processor.

Welsh Rarebit

3 *fl. oz. stale beer (milk may*   *dash Worcestershire sauce*
  be substituted)   *pinch each paprika, pepper*
1 *oz. butter*   1 *egg yolk (optional)*
6 *oz. Cheddar cheese, grated*   2 *tablespoons lecithin*
1 *teaspoon prepared mustard*

Warm the beer or milk with the butter. Add all the other ingredients and stir until smooth.

Pour the cheese mixture over toasted bread and grill until brown and bubbly.

Serves 2.

Macaroni and Cheese Casserole

$\frac{1}{2}$ *lb. whole wheat macaroni*   1 *oz. wheat germ*
1 *oz. butter*   2   *tablespoons powdered*
2 *oz. whole wheat flour*   *lecithin*
$\frac{1}{4}$ *teaspoon powdered mustard*   *salt and pepper to taste*
$1\frac{1}{4}$ *pints skimmed milk*   *wheat germ*
8 *oz. sharp cheese, grated*   *paprika*

Cook the macaroni in boiling salted water until just done. Drain, save the water for soup.

Heat oven to 375°F.

Melt the butter in a large saucepan. Stir in the flour to mix well, stir in the mustard and the milk, and cook, stirring until thickened. Turn off the heat, and in the cheese, $\frac{1}{2}$ cup wheat germ and lecithin. Taste for seasoning.

Place the cooked macaroni in a large, oiled casserole, and pour the cheese sauce over it. Sprinkle the top with a little wheat germ and paprika.

Bake about 30 minutes or until golden and bubbly.

Serves 6.

Colourful Quiche

PASTRY

6 *oz. whole wheat flour*   1 *egg*

2 *fl. oz. peanut oil*   1 *to* 3 *tablespoons cold milk*

FILLING

1 *tablespoon oil*   3 *eggs*

1 *large onion, finely diced*   6 *oz. natural yogurt*

salt and pepper to taste   2   *tablespoons   powdered*

½ *cup grated Emmenthaler or*   *lecithin*

   Gruyere cheese   1 *small tomato, sliced thinly*

1 *oz. freshly grated Parmesan*

   cheese

Mix the flour, peanut oil and egg for the pastry. Add the milk, a tablespoon at a time, to make a cohesive pastry. Pat the pastry to cover the bottom and sides of a 9″ flan tin.

Heat oven to 350°F.

Heat the 1 tablespoon oil and sauté the onion until it is soft. Sprinkle the onion over the crust, dust with salt and pepper to taste, then sprinkle with the cheeses. Beat the eggs lightly and stir in the yogurt and lecithin. Pour over the cheeses, and top with the sliced tomato. Bake 45–50 minutes or until lightly browned.

Best served lukewarm, but can be hot or cold.

Eggs

Eggs are one of the world's most beautiful foods. They are delightfully packaged, and are also a marvellous source of protein. In fact, one dozen eggs averages about one and one-half pounds of economical, high-quality protein, as well as vitamins and minerals. The white of an egg, which comprises about 58 percent of the total weight, contains albumen (protein) and minerals. The yolk contains some albumen plus vitamins, lecithines, nucleines, cholesterines and minerals. The yolk is about 30 percent of the total weight of an egg, while the shell is about 12 percent.

There has been a lot of controversy and panic about eggs and cholesterol. Since egg yolks contain cholesterol, eggs have been restricted in many diets. The *facts* are these: While an egg contains 275 milligrams of cholesterol, the average human body *manufactures* up to 2,000 milligrams *per day!* Furthermore, eggs also contain lecithin, which acts as a solvent on cholesterol. Actually, only about 5 percent of the population cannot tolerate additional cholesterol or saturated fat. (Eggs contain five grams of saturated fat, three grams of unsaturated fat.) For the rest of us, eggs are a delicious, nourishing food which deserves an important place in our diets.

The actual nutritional content of a 50 gram egg is 6.3 grams of protein, 5.6 grams of fat, .95 grams of carbohydrate, 27 milligrams of calcium, 102 milligrams of phosphorous, 1.5 milligrams of iron, 61 milligrams of sodium, 64 milligrams of potassium, 590 I.U. of Vitamin A, .05 milligrams of thiamin, .15 milligrams of riboflavin, .05 milligrams of niacin and 5.5 grams of magnesium. All that for only 80 calories!

Eggs do not keep well unless refrigerated and they also

absorb odours and flavours through pores in the shell so, if possible, they should be stored away from strong smelling substances. The fresher the egg the better it tastes so obviously it is best to buy free-range eggs from a farm or health-food shop. If this is impossible, there are effectively only two grades of egg available in shops in this country. The freshest, and therefore best, are packaged in containers with a red band around bearing the word "Extra". The red band must, under EEC regulations, be destroyed not later than the seventh day after packing so, if you are fortunate enough to find them, you can be sure they are very fresh. However, the majority of eggs found on supermarket shelves are Class A. To check the freshness of an unbroken egg, hold it up to a light so that the inside can be seen. The yolk should appear without apparent contours, and should not appear to be moving perceptibly from its central position when the egg is rotated. It should also be free from any kind of foreign substance. When broken, a fresh egg will have an upstanding yolk, thick albumen (white) layer surrounding it and a more liquid outer albumen layer. Class B eggs are not available for sale in the retail trade in Britain.

Eggs range in size from Size 1 – Size 7. For boiling or poaching, Sizes 1 (70 grams or over) or 2 (65–70 grams) are best. We do not specify the egg size in the recipes in this book because, while we have been working with Size 2 eggs, Size 1 or 3 would give similar results.

Many refrigerator doors have shelves with little pockets into which one is supposed to put eggs. Unfortunately, that is not a very good place to store them. Eggshells are porous, and eggs should be refrigerated in COVERED cartons, with the large end up so that the air pocket will help to preserve the egg. If you are lucky enough to have a refrigerator with an egg *drawer*, store them in that, other wise, turn the eggs large end up and store them in the original carton. Don't wash eggs until they are about to be used, as washing removes a natural protective coating, and will hasten spoilage. Farm fresh eggs will keep for about 5 weeks. Cooked eggs in the shell will keep about 10 days, but shelled, only about 3 days. Yolks will keep about a week if they are covered with water. To use them, simply pour off the water. Whites may be kept in a covered container for about a week. They may also be frozen for up to 6 months.

To save money (and your temper) break eggs one at a time into a small bowl. That way, if you get a bad egg, it may be discarded without having to throw out all the other eggs. If you are separating eggs, have them very cold. Break them one at a time into a small bowl, then pour the egg into your hand, and let the white run out between your fingers. Messy, but it works well. To beat egg whites, be sure that there is no fat or oil on the bowl or beaters, and no speck of egg yolk among the whites. If you do get yolk in the whites, just spoon it out. To aid in the beating, add $\frac{1}{8}$ teaspoon of cream of tartar for each white.

Soft-Boiled Eggs

Cover the eggs with cold water, cover the pan and cook until the water boils. Depending on the degree of softness desired, remove the eggs immediately, or let them stand in the water for up to 4 minutes.

Hard-Boiled Eggs

Cover the eggs with cold water, cover the pan and cook until the water boils, simmer 1 or 2 minutes, let stand off heat for 20 minutes. Drain and chill immediately in cold water. For soft yolks, let stand only four to eight minutes.

Poached Eggs

Use the freshest possible eggs. Heat water to boiling in a large shallow pan. Break the eggs one at a time into a small bowl, and slip one at a time into the water. Some cooks prefer to stir the water to make a tiny whirlpool and drop the egg into the centre of it. Remove the pan from the heat and let stand 10 minutes. If you are in a hurry, you may simmer the eggs for 5 minutes. Remove the eggs with a slotted spoon. You can also poach eggs in milk. Place the poached eggs on toast and pour the milk over.

Basic Soufflé

Oil	*½ cup cooked leftover veget-*
1 *tablespoon grated Parmesan*	*ables, meat or cheese (well*
cheese	*flavoured)*
1½ *oz. butter*	*½ teaspoon salt*
2 *oz. whole wheat flour*	*½ teaspoon cream of tartar*
1 *cup milk*	4 *egg whites*
4 *egg yolks*	*salt and pepper to taste*

Heat oven to 375°F.

Oil a 2 pint soufflé dish or charlotte mould. Sprinkle with the Parmesan cheese.

Melt the butter in a saucepan, add the flour and stir one minute. Add the milk and salt and pepper to taste. Cook, stirring constantly, until sauce is thick and smooth. Remove from heat. Stir in the egg yolks, one at a time, mixing well. Add the vegetables, meat or cheese to the yolk mixture.

Beat the egg whites with the salt and cream of tartar to form stiff peaks. Stir about ¼ of the beaten whites into the yolk mixture, fold in the remaining whites. Pour the mixture into the soufflé dish. Smooth the top.

Bake 35–40 minutes or until the soufflé is puffed and golden.

Serves 4.

Eggs Creole

2 *tablespoons oil*	1 *oz. whole wheat flour*
1 *small onion, chopped*	2 *cups tinned tomatoes*
1 *stalk celery, chopped*	1 *teaspoon salt*
1 *green pepper, chopped*	¾ *teaspoon chili powder*

4–6 *hard-boiled eggs, peeled*
  and chopped

Heat the oil and sauté the onion, celery and pepper until soft. Stir in the flour. Add the tomatoes, salt and chili powder and cook to make a thick sauce. You may add a little water if the sauce becomes too thick. Add the eggs and stir gently to heat through.

Serve on whole wheat toast.

Serves 4.

Curried Eggs

2 *tablespoons oil*
1 *carrot, grated*
1 *onion, minced*
1 *apple, cored and grated*
1 *oz. whole wheat flour*
1 *oz. curry powder*

8 *fl. oz. stock, milk or water*
1 *tablespoon lemon juice*
salt to taste
4–6 *hard-boiled eggs, shelled*
  and chopped

Heat the oil and sauté the carrot, onion and apple until soft. Stir in the flour and curry powder. Gradually stir in the liquid. Cook about 5 minutes, or until the sauce is thick. Add lemon juice and salt to taste. Add the chopped eggs just to heat through.

Serve over cooked brown rice.

Serves 4.

Omelets

An omelet calls for 4 ingredients: absolutely fresh eggs, very good butter, an omelet pan, and the cook's entire attention. Omelets cook very quickly, and distraction can be ruinous! An omelet pan is rounded or sloping where the sides and bottom join. It should be heavy enough to distribute the heat evenly. The un-glamorous French iron pans are fine, and the size we prefer is one with a bottom about 6 inches in diameter. The largest omelet that can be made in this size is a three-egg omelet, and we generally confine ourselves to two.

An omelet pan must be seasoned. Wash the new pan very well and dry it. Heat it until it is just too hot to touch, then rub the entire inner surface with vegetable oil. Leave it alone overnight. Heat it as before, rub it with oil, and wipe away all of the excess. The pan should never be washed again. After use it should be wiped with a dry cloth or paper towel. If something sticks to the pan, rub it away with salt.

Plain Omelet for One

2 *eggs*
½ *oz. butter*

Stir the eggs in a small bowl just until they are mixed. Heat the pan over medium heat. When the pan is hot, add the butter. Swirl the butter around to cover the pan. When the butter stops foaming, add the eggs all at once. Holding the pan firmly in your left hand, stir the eggs rapidly with a fork, keeping the tines parallel with the bottom of the pan. In about 4 seconds the eggs will begin to set. Smooth the still liquid eggs across the top to fill any holes. Lift the edges of the omelet with the fork, and tipping the pan away from you, fold the omelet in half, give the pan a shake, moving the omelet into the centre of the pan.

Grasp the handle of the pan in your right hand, and a warm plate in your left hand. Hold the plate at a 45 degree angle and tip the pan against it, also at a 45 degree angle. Quickly invert the pan over the plate, and the omelet will flip onto the plate.

The whole operation should take about 30 seconds. For several people, we like to make successive omelets, keeping them warm in a very low oven (115°F.), if necessary.

Filled Omelets

Fillings are the best part of omelet making. Almost anything can be tucked in, from leftovers to freshly sautéed mushrooms, grated cheese, crumbled bacon, or one of our favourites — sliced bananas sprinkled with wheat germ and a dash of cinnamon.

Have your filling ready to hand. Prepare the omelet as for a plain omelet up to the point where you are ready to fold the omelet. At this point, place a line of filling across the omelet, just a little further away from centre. *Now* fold the omelet and proceed as above.

Baked Eggs

8 *eggs*
vegetable oil

1 *oz. grated mature Cheddar*
 cheese
½ *teaspoon lecithin powder*

Heat oven to 325°F.

Oil baking dishes or custard cups that will hold 2 eggs each. Break 2 eggs into each dish. Top the eggs with the cheese and lecithin.

Bake the eggs for about 10 minutes or until they are as "set" as you like.

For variety, add chopped fresh herbs.

Serves 4.

Eggs Florentine

4 *cups chopped, cooked spinach*
2 *oz. butter*
2 *shallots, minced (or 2 tablespoons minced onion)*
3 *tablespoons whole wheat flour*

12 *fl. oz. skimmed milk*
2 *tablespoons powdered lecithin*
salt and pepper to taste
8 *eggs*
¼ *cup grated Parmesan cheese*
paprika

Heat the spinach and keep it warm. Melt the butter and sauté the shallots until they are just becoming translucent. Stir in the flour and mix well, then stir in the milk and the lecithin and cook the sauce, stirring until it has thickened. Season to taste.

Drain the spinach, reserving the liquid, and return the spinach to the pan. Add to it half of the sauce. Cook and stir until it is well mixed. If it seems very thick, add some of the spinach liquid. (Save the remainder for soup.)

Poach the eggs.

Spread the spinach mixture in a large serving dish. Arrange the eggs on the spinach. Top the eggs with the remaining sauce. Sprinkle on the Parmesan, and add a few dashes of paprika for garnish.

If you have the time, the inclination, and an ovenproof dish, you can slip the finished dish under the grill for a minute or two to brown.

Serves 4.

Eggs Foo Yong

6 *fl. oz. water*
1 *teaspoon tomato paste*
2 *tablespoons soy sauce*
$\frac{1}{2}$ *teaspoon honey*
1 *tablespoon cornflour mixed with 2 tablespoons cold water*

3 *spring onions, minced (separate white and green parts)*
6 *eggs, lightly beaten*
1 *cup steamed soy sprouts*
$\frac{1}{4}$ *teaspoon salt*
$\frac{1}{3}$ *cup minced, cooked meat or poultry (optional)*
vegetable oil

Bring the water to a boil. Add the tomato paste, soy sauce and honey. Add the cornflour mixture to the boiling liquid, while stirring. Remove from heat and stir in the green part of the spring onions. Keep warm.

Mix together the eggs, white of onions, salt, soy sprouts and meat.

Heat a little oil in a wok or small frying pan. Add about one sixth of the egg mixture. Let cook until done on the bottom, then turn and cook the other side. Remove to a dish and keep warm. Continue similarly until all of the egg mixture has been used. Pour the warm sauce over the cooked egg patties and serve warm.

Serves 6.

Asparagus-Lemon Omelets

4 *eggs*
4 *teaspoons fresh lemon juice*
12–16 *tender asparagus spears*
½ *oz. butter*
½ *cup unseasoned béchamel sauce*
1 *teaspoon Dijon-type mustard*
dash Tabasco

Beat two eggs lightly and add ½ teaspoon lemon juice. In a separate bowl, repeat with the remaining two eggs.

Trim the asparagus stems and poach the spears in boiling water until just tender-crisp. Keep warm.

Heat the béchamel sauce and beat in the mustard, Tabasco and lemon juice. Keep warm.

Fill each omelet with a ribbon of sauce and ¼ of the asparagus. Garnish with ¼ of the asparagus and more sauce.

"Soft" Eggs

1 *egg, in the shell*
cider vinegar

This recipe produces a soft-shelled egg which may be used, *shell and all*, to make egg-nogs and mayonnaise. Simply place the egg in a small container, and cover with the vinegar. Let stand 8–12 hours. The vinegar will be less sharp. Skim and use for salads.

Super Eggs

½ *small tomato, cup up and*
  skinned
¼ *small onion, cut up*
½ *oz. soy flour*
1 *tablespoon plain yogurt*
2 *teaspoons wheat germ*

2 *teaspoons nutritional yeast*
2 *eggs*
½ *teaspoon chili powder*
pinch salt
oil

Mix all ingredients except oil in a blender until well mixed.

Heat oil in a large frying pan. Add the egg mixture and stir gently until done to taste.

Serves 1.

Creamed Hard-Boiled Eggs

1 *oz. butter*
2 *tablespoons oil*
1 *stalk celery, finely diced*
1 *medium onion, finely diced*
½ *cup sliced mushrooms*
1 *teaspoon chopped pimiento,*
  or fresh red pepper
2 *oz. whole wheat flour*

16 *fl. oz. skimmed milk*
1 *oz. Parmesan cheese, grated*
1 *teaspoon salt*
6 *hard-boiled eggs, chopped*
Parmesan cheese to garnish
1 *hard-boiled egg, sliced*
cooked whole wheat or spinach
  noodles

Heat the butter and oil in a heavy pot. Stir in the celery and onion until they are becoming translucent, then add the mushrooms and sauté until they are becoming limp. Add the pimiento, then the flour. Stir until the flour is well mixed. Stir in the milk, cheese and salt. Cook over gentle heat, stirring, until the sauce thickens. Add the six chopped hard-boiled eggs and cook just to heat them through.

Pour the egg mixture over the noodles, garnish with the sliced egg and a sprinkle of Parmesan cheese.

Serves 6.

Eggs Mornay with Prawns

2 cups chopped, cooked prawns
2 oz. butter
1½ oz. flour
14 fl. oz. milk
1 cup grated cheddar-type cheese
¼ cup grated Parmesan
½ teaspoon dry mustard
2 tablespoons powdered lecithin
½ teaspoon salt
dash white pepper
2 tablespoons dry sherry
8 eggs

Melt the butter in a heavy saucepan. When it has ceased to foam, stir in the flour until well mixed, then add the milk. Let cook for about 5 minutes, stirring, until the sauce is thickened. Remove from the heat and add the cheeses, mustard, lecithin and seasoning. Keep warm.

Poach the eggs.

While the eggs are poaching, heat the sherry in a small pan. When it is hot, touch it with a lighted match and let it flame until all the alcohol has burned away. Stir in the prawns. Drain the prawns.

Divide the prawns onto 4 warm plates. Place two poached eggs over the prawns on each plate, and top with the Mornay sauce. If you can run the dishes briefly under a grill to brown, so much the better.

Variation: Use crabmeat instead of prawns.

Serves 4.

Tomato Scramble

2 tomatoes, peeled, seeded and chopped
1 teaspoon minced chives
1 teaspoon minced parsley
pinch salt
dash pepper
1 oz. butter
2 tablespoons sunflower oil
12 eggs lightly beaten

Heat ½ oz. of the butter and 1 tablespoon sunflower oil and sauté the tomatoes, chives, parsley, salt and pepper until just warmed, about two minutes. Set aside.

In a large frying pan, heat the remaining oil and butter. Add the eggs and stir until they are soft and just beginning to set. Stir in the tomato mixture.
Serves 6.

Yogurt

Yogurt can be made from goat, sheep, cow's milk or soy milk and an organism called *lactobacillus bulgaricus*. This organism or culture ferments the milk, producing a thickened, tangy wonder-food called yogurt. It has all the potassium, phosphorous and calcium of milk but it is digestible by people who cannot tolerate milk! Yogurt is 90 percent digestible within one hour, as compared to 30 percent for plain milk. Yogurt is reputed to have a very beneficial action on the intestinal flora, not only in aiding digestion, but actually producing the friendly bacteria that are conducive to intestinal well-being. Balkan peoples for whom yogurt is an everyday food, attribute their longevity to it! Yogurt in many forms is available in most supermarkets but if you don't read the label carefully, you might get something you don't really want! There is *nothing* in yogurt except milk and the yogurt culture — anything else is an additive. Fruit yogurt contains fruit preserves, which make it taste good but contain white sugar. Yogurt *on* fruit or made with honey and fruit is scrumptious! If you find anything on the label that shouldn't be there, look for another brand. A lot of dairies are selling ersatz yogurt in order to cash in on its growing popularity but there are many reliable, honest brands to choose from. Yogurt is delicious plain, and its tangy taste blends well with both fruits and vegetables. Cooking yogurt destroys the culture, so it is most valuable raw. However, the food value and good taste make it a delectable ingredient in cooked dishes as well.

Making your own yogurt is a simple affair. You need only milk, a "starter" culture and a warm place where the culture can grow. The warm place can be a yogurt maker, most of which make four to five cups of yogurt at a time very reliably. Our oven, which has a pilot light, incubates yogurt very efficiently. A hot pad which maintains the right temperature will make as many containers of yogurt as will fit into a cardboard box lined with the heating pad and topped with a thick towel. It's not elegant but it works! Any investment in a yogurt maker will probably pay for itself many times over. Even if you don't have a handy cow, you can make yogurt from non-instant dried milk, which is available in most health food stores, at a small price. The starter culture for your yogurt may be obtained from any good, plain yogurt, or from a dried culture. The dried culture may seem expensive but it makes a batch of starter which may be frozen and used over many months, making it actually most economical. No starter will last indefinitely. After several batches, your yogurt will not thicken readily and the starter must be replaced. We need a new batch of starter every month, making yogurt at least once a week.

Different starter cultures and different milks produce different flavours of yogurt. Depending on many mysterious imponderables, yogurt also differs in thickness and texture from batch to batch. The first batch may take up to eight hours to "make," while succeeding batches may only take three or four hours, except in summer, when it seems to take longer. Yogurt making is an adventure!

Yogurt may be flavoured with honey, preserves, fruit or any flavouring you'd like to try. Just stir it into the milk after it has been heated (see below). We prefer plain yogurt but the children like honey yogurt, too. If you have only tried plain yogurt from the store, you may be pleasantly surprised at the different flavour (milder, nuttier) of homemade yogurt.

The recipe we are giving for making your own yogurt is the one that involves the least investment. When you are really into yogurt making, you can shop around for the equipment that suits you best. Yogurt makers all come with instructions but here is the basic recipe:

Yogurt

1½ *pints milk*   1 *small container plain yogurt*
                        (if you are using dried cul-
                        ture, follow package direc-
                        tions)

Heat the milk to 180°F. Let it cool to about 110°F.

Let the yogurt come to room temperature while the milk is cooling.

When the milk reaches 110°F. stir in the yogurt. Put the mixture in a warmed glass, stoneware or enamelled cast iron container with a lid. (Please don't use earthenware which may have a low-fired lead glaze. Yogurt is acid and may release lead.) Wrap the container in a large terry towel and put the whole thing in a warm place for 4 to 8 hours until it is set. Try not to disturb your yogurt too much when you check on it. Rock the container very slightly. The yogurt will get very thick, even custardy, depending on its temperament. Refrigerate the yogurt when it is done.

If you are hunting for a place in which to keep your yogurt warm, consider any place where you can successfully set bread to rise. Think about a large-mouth thermos. Try a heating pad with a thermostatic control.

Yogurt Drinks

Since yogurt liquifies when it is stirred, it becomes a base for many refreshing drinks. Plain, it is a little like buttermilk, but better. If you like it sweet, stir in a little honey or whirl it in the blender with honey and fresh fruit. We like it mixed with tomato juice and also with cucumbers that have been liquified in the blender and a dash of cumin. Be creative! Experiment! Just don't forget to save a half a cup as a starter for your next batch.

Yogurt Cheese

One cup of yogurt makes about one third of a cup of

cheese. Place a large square of cheesecloth over a colander. Place the yogurt in the centre of the cheesecloth and twist the cloth to cover the yogurt. Suspend the cheesecloth where it will drain and let drain for about 12 hours. The result will be similar to soft cream cheese. Mix it with finely chopped chives, herbs or nuts for a spread for bread or a filling for celery sticks. You can thin it a little with plain yogurt and use it as a dip for raw vegetables.

Seafare

There is a wealth of good food to be found in the sea. Fish are an important economic resource to coastal populations all over the world, and inventive ways have been found to use an enormous variety of fish and shellfish. Fish are available tinned, smoked, salted and dried, as well as fresh and frozen. For those of us not fortunate enough to live near a seacoast, modern transportation provides a vast array of seafare from which to choose.

Fish are a delicious, economical source of high-quality protein. Because the flesh of fish contains little connective tissue, the protein is easily digested and assimilated. Almost all parts of a fish may be used. Heads and bones are used to make delicious stocks, so there is very little waste. Fish are also a good source of B vitamins and a rich source of minerals. They are rish in calcium, iron, potassium, phosphorus, copper, iron, manganese, cobalt and other trace minerals. Most shellfish contain magnesium, and oysters are a rich source of zinc. Most fish are relatively low in fat. Fatty-fleshed fish are rich in Vitamins A and D.

Fish are available either whole, or in fillets and steaks. When buying fresh fish, look for firm flesh, a clean non-fishy odour, bright, clear protruding eyes, red gills and shiny skin. If the fish has been cut into fillets or steaks look for firm flesh with no signs of drying and a clean odour. Frozen fish should have a natural, bright colour with no signs of discolouration or dryness; and should be tightly wrapped with no signs of air spaces or loose wrapping. Fish should not be allowed to stand at room temperature for more than two hours, and frozen fish should thaw in the refrigerator. Fish may be cooked frozen, if extra time for thawing is allowed.

When buying fish, plan portions as follows for each serving:

Whole fish	$\frac{3}{4}$ pound
Dressed fish	$\frac{1}{2}$ pound
Fillets or steaks	$\frac{1}{3}$ pound

Fresh fish should not be kept in the refrigerator for more than two days. Fresh fish may be frozen, but fish that has been frozen and thawed should not be refrozen.

One of the joys of cooking fish is that it cooks rather quickly. Whether you fry, bake, grill, poach or steam your fish, you should pay attention to its degree of doneness. As soon as the flesh flakes easily with a fork, the fish is done and should not be cooked any further. Fish is at its most delicious when its natural moisture is retained. Shellfish are cooked when the flesh changes colour and become opaque. Overcooking results in tough shellfish. Often, the simplest cooking methods are the best for fish. Simple poaching in water to which a bit of white wine has been added can produce a delicately flavourful fish which needs only a bit of lemon juice for garnish.

If you have leftover fish, you can use it in a variety of ways. Chill the fish and remove the skin and bones. Flake the flesh and use it in salads, omelets, crepes or fish cakes. Mix the flakes with a little tartar sauce for a delightful sandwich. Add flakes to flavoured cream sauce with sautéed mushrooms and cooked macaroni for a quick casserole supper.

Great Day for Banana Fish

fish fillets for 6 *people*	3 *bananas*
3–4 *tablespoons oil*	*butter or oil*
$\frac{1}{2}$ *large lemon*	2 *tablespoons pine nuts*

Pre-heat the grill.

In a shallow baking dish, roll the fillets in the 3–4 tablespoons oil until they are coated. Sprinkle them with the juice of $\frac{1}{2}$ lemon. Peel the bananas, halve them lengthwise and cut them into large pieces. Arrange the banana on the fillets. Dot with butter or sprinkle with oil and grill until the bananas are just beginning to brown, and the fish is nearly done. Sprinkle the pine nuts on the dish and grill a few seconds more, until they are lightly browned.

Serves 6.

Pineapple Fish Casserole

1 *lb. plaice fillets*	2 *teaspoons cornflour*
6 *slices tinned pineapple*	$\frac{1}{2}$ *cup pineapple juice*
1 *leek, or two spring onions,*	1 *egg*
chopped	$\frac{1}{2}$ *teaspoon salt*

Oil a 2-pint casserole. Heat oven to 350°F.

Arrange the fish in the bottom of the casserole, top with the pineapple slices and the chopped leek.

Mix the cornflour into the pineapple juice to make a smooth mixture. Beat in the egg and the salt. Pour the mixture over the fish. Bake at 350°F. for 30 minutes, or until lightly browned. (The fish should be flaky and opaque.)

Serves 4.

Special Grilled Fillets

fish fillets for 6 people	*dash pepper*
2 *oz. toasted wheat germ*	1 *teaspoon salt (optional)*
1 *teaspoon paprika*	2 *tablespoons lemon juice*
$\frac{1}{2}$ *teaspoon powdered garlic*	2 *tablespoons oil*
(optional)	4–5 *fat mushrooms, sliced*

Pre-heat a grill.

Mix together the wheat germ, paprika, garlic, pepper and salt. Roll the fillets in the mixture to coat, and place them in a well-oiled, shallow baking dish. Mix the lemon juice with the oil and sprinkle it over the fish. Grill for a

minute or two, then turn the fillets over. Sprinkle on any leftover wheatgerm mixture, and add the mushrooms. Return the dish to the grill and continue cooking until done.
Serves 6.

Fantastic Fish Pie

1½ *lb. potatoes, unpeeled*	¼ *lb. mushrooms, sliced*
2 *lbs. whole fish (cleaned and scaled)*	1 *small onion, chopped finely*
	2 *tablespoons fresh, chopped parsley*
8 *fl. oz milk*	
1 *onion, in chunks*	1 *oz. whole wheat flour*
1 *teaspoon salt*	1 *teaspoon salt*
pinch thyme	*dash white pepper*
milk (more)	½ *teaspoon paprika*
2 *tablespoons oil*	2 *tablespoons sherry (optional)*
½ *oz. butter*	1 *tablespoon wheat germ*

Boil the potatoes in salted water until done.

While the potatoes are cooking, heat the 8 fl. oz milk, onion in chunks, 1 teaspoon salt, thyme and add the fish. Poach gently 5 to 10 minutes or until fish is done. Let cool. Strain the milk and reserve. Flake the fish and remove all bones and skin.

Mash the potatoes or force them through a food mill. Oil a deep 9 inch baking dish and line it with a potato "crust." Heat oven to 350°F.

Add milk to the reserved milk to make a total of 12 fl. oz. Heat the oil and butter, and sauté the mushrooms, chopped onion and parsley. Stir in the flour and cook 2–3 minutes, stirring. Add the salt, pepper, paprika and milk. Cook slowly until thickened. Stir in the flaked fish and sherry and pour the mixture into the potato "shell". Bake at 350°F. for 45 minutes or until brown. Sprinkle with wheat germ.
Serves 6.

Stuffed Mussels

3 *dozen large mussels (about)*
16 *fl. oz. dry white wine*
1 *large clove garlic, minced*
¼ *teaspoon each thyme, orega-*
 no, pepper
2 *tablespoons oil*
4–5 *shallots, minced (*1
 med. onion may be substi-
 tuted)

½ *green pepper, minced*
1 *oz. whole wheat flour*
¾ *cup whole wheat bread*
 crumbs
butter
parsley

Scrub the mussels well and place them in a pan with the wine, garlic, thyme, oregano and pepper. Cover the pan and keep liquid at simmer until the mussels open. Those that won't open at all should be discarded. Remove the mussels with a slotted spoon and set aside to cool, halving shells. Discard empty half. Strain the broth through a cloth and boil it until it is reduced to 12 fl. oz.

Heat the oil and cook the shallots and pepper until the shallots are translucent. Stir in the flour and crumbs, and gradually add the broth, stirring. Cook and stir until it is thick. Heat the grill.

Top each mussel with a dollop of shallot/pepper sauce and a dot of butter. Grill until browned. Garnish with parsley.

Serves 4–6 as an appetizer, 2–3 as a main course.

Basic Boiled Shrimp or Prawns

shrimps or prawns in their
 shells
water to cover
1 *teaspoon salt*

1 *leafy stalk celery*
1 *small onion*
½ *lemon (peel, seeds and all)*

Heat the water to a boil, add the salt, celery, onion and lemon. Return to a full rolling boil and drop in the shrimp. In about **ONE MINUTE** they will become opaque and pink. Drain immediately and rinse with cold water to stop the cooking.

Prawns Louis

4 *cups cold boiled prawns, shelled*
1 *head lettuce, preferably Cos*
2 *tablespoons piccallilli**
2 *tablespoons ketchup**
1 *teaspoon Worcestershire sauce*

1 *small green pepper, chopped finely*
2 *small spring onions, chopped*
2 *teaspoons pimiento, chopped (optional)*
2 *tablespoons lemon juice*
salt and pepper to taste
1 *cup yogurt*

* For recipes, see pages 194 and 196.

Arrange the prawns on the lettuce, reserving a few prawns for garnish. You may use a large platter or individual plates.

Mix together the piccallilli, ketchup, Worcestershire sauce, pepper, spring onions, pimiento and lemon juice. Stir into the yogurt, a little at a time, until the sauce is as thick or thin as you like. Pour the sauce over the prawns. Garnish with the reserved prawns.

Serves 4.

Red Mullet Des Mareyeurs

2–4 *large mullet fillets*
salt and pepper to taste
1 *tablespoon chopped parsley*
2 *shallots, minced*
1 *tablespoon Dijon mustard*

¼ *cup dry white wine*
1 *teaspoon lemon juice*
2 *tablespoons butter*
parsley for garnish

Heat oven to 325°F. Arrange fish in a buttered baking dish and sprinkle with salt and pepper. Sprinkle on the chopped parsley and shallots. Mix the mustard with the wine

and pour over the fish. Bake 30 minutes. Remove the fish from the oven and keep warm. Raise oven temperature to 350°F. Pour sauce from fish into a saucepan and stir over high heat until sauce is reduced by one-third. Add lemon juice and butter. Heat and stir until butter is melted. Pour sauce over fish. Return dish to oven and bake until golden brown.
Serves 2–4.

Moules Marinieres

This is what we like to do at the beach, but you should know a lot about mussels before you go a-gathering, as some are inedible, and they are prey to some pollutants.

4 *lbs. mussels, scrubbed and debearded*
6 *shallots or two cloves garlic, minced*
1 *bay leaf*

½ *teaspoon freshly ground pepper*
2 *cups dry white wine (water may be used)*

Put everything together in a large pot. Set the pot over a nice, hot fire, cover it tightly, and steam the mussels for about 5 minutes. When the mussels are open, they are done. Serve the mussels in bowls. The broth may be strained through a cloth and drunk, or sopped up with whole-wheat French bread. Delicious!
Serves 4.

Hangtown Fry

10–12 *shelled oysters*
whole wheat flour
1 *tablespoon butter*
2 *tablespoons oil*

1 *spring onion, chopped*
salt and pepper
6 *eggs, well beaten*
2 *tablespoons cream*

Dust the oysters with flour. Heat the oil and butter and fry the oysters until golden. Add the spring onion and mix well. Sprinkle with salt and pepper. Mix the eggs with the cream and pour over the oysters. Cook until eggs are set, lifting frequently to let the soft part of the eggs run underneath.

Serves 2.

Baked Fish with Tomato Sauce

3½ lbs. firm, dry-fleshed fish, filleted
¼ lb. butter
1 teaspoon salt

¼ teaspoon pepper
⅓ cup lemon juice
¼ cup dry white wine

SAUCE

2 tablespoons oil
1 medium size onion, chopped
2 cloves garlic, crushed
3 medium tomatoes, peeled, seeded and chopped

8 fl. oz. dry white wine
8 fl. oz. water
1 bay leaf
salt and pepper to taste
1 oz. whole wheat flour

Heat oven to 350°F. Arrange fish in a shallow baking dish. Mix together the butter, salt, pepper, lemon juice and wine. Heat until butter is melted. Pour butter mixture over fish and bake for about 40 minutes or until fish is done, basting once or twice if needed.

Meanwhile, heat the oil and sauté the onion and garlic until soft. Add the tomatoes, 8 fl. oz wine, water and bay leaf. Cook 20 minutes. Season with salt and pepper. Add some of the sauce to the flour and mix until smooth, then return the flour mixture to the simmering sauce, stirring constantly until sauce is thickened. Force the sauce through a food mill or purée in a blender. Keep sauce warm.

Serve fish in its baking dish with the sauce in a separate sauceboat.

Serves 6.

Scampi

2 lbs. large Dublin Bay prawns, shelled and de-veined
4 fl. oz. olive oil
2 cloves garlic, minced
2 teaspoons salt
½ cup parsley, chopped
lemon wedges
hot, cooked brown rice

Leave tails on prawns, if possible. Arrange them in a shallow baking dish. Mix olive oil with garlic, salt and half of the parsley. Pour mixture over fish. Grill about 4 inches from the heat until thoroughly cooked, turning and basting as they cook.

Pour prawns and sauce over rice. Garnish with remaining parsley and lemon wedges.

Serves 4.

Oyster Loaf

1 loaf whole wheat French bread
1 clove garlic, peeled and cut in half
salt and pepper to taste
dash Tabasco sauce
dash Worcestershire sauce
2 eggs, lightly beaten
6–12 fresh, drained oysters per person
2 oz. whole wheat flour
2 oz. soy flour
1 cup whole wheat bread crumbs
2 tablespoons oil
1 tablespoon butter

Cut the top off the bread to form a lid. Hollow the lid and the bottom. Place the bread in a low oven until crisp. Rub the inside of the loaf with the cut garlic.

Add the salt and pepper, Tabasco and Worcestershire sauce to the eggs. Mix the whole wheat flour with the soy flour. Dip the oysters in the flour mixture, then into the eggs, then into the crumbs. Sauté the oysters in the oil and butter until crisp. Fill the hollow loaf with oysters. Replace the lid and keep warm in an oven until ready to serve.

Crab Sauté

1 *stalk celery, chopped finely*
6–7 *mushrooms, chopped finely*
½ *medium onion, chopped finely*
1 *teaspoon minced chives*
2 *tablespoons butter*

3 *tablespoons fresh lemon juice*
¾ *cup crabmeat (cooked or tinned may be used)*
2 *slices whole wheat toast, cut into triangles*

Stir the celery, mushrooms, onion and chives in the butter over medium heat until they are becoming translucent. Add the lemon juice and the crabmeat, cover the pot and steam over very low heat for about 5 minutes or until the crab is cooked through.

Serve over toast points.

Serves 2.

Corn-Oyster Casserole

1⅔ *cups cream style sweetcorn (17 oz. tin)*
2 *cup dry whole wheat bread crumbs*
1 *egg beaten*
4 *fl. oz. skimmed milk*
2 *tablespoons oil*

1 *teaspoon salt*
1 *oz. wheat germ*
¼ *cup minced green pepper*
2 *tablespoons soy flour*
1 *pint small fresh oysters, drained*
dash pepper

Heat oven to 350°F. Oil a casserole.

Mix all ingredients together. Pour into the prepared casserole and bake 30 minutes or until set.

Serves 4–6.

Meat and Poultry

Long regarded as unbeatable sources of high-quality protein, meat and poultry are rapidly losing favour for a number of reasons, chief among them the high demand for meat. Meat is traditionally a major part of the British diet.

Small farms can produce small herds of cattle on land that is virtually unusable for anything else. Grain in amounts too small to be marketable can be raised as cattle feed, and when the cornfields are lying fallow, cattle can graze there. Formerly farmers raised cattle this way, and used some of the grain for their families' flour. Obviously, we cannot raise enough beef this way to feed even a small town, and in our meat-hungry nation, cattle raising has become big business. Calves are immobilized in pens and fed synthetic vitamins, hormones and antibiotics with feed planned to maximize their weight gain in the shortest possible time. They are a chemical feast, indeed! Their feed is grown in the same mega-business fashion, artificially fertilized, sprayed, gassed, and doused with pesticide. The pesticide residues eventually concentrate in the fat of those super-fat animals.

Pigs, lambs, chickens, turkeys, etc., fare as poorly as the cattle. Chickens are grown in "factories" where they are kept in little cages to they can't run around and get skinny, they can only sit and eat the feed that goes by on a conveyer belt. A little dash of arsenic in the feed makes their skin appetizingly yellow! Nearly all of our meat and poultry is grown in little boxes — an obviously unhealthy environment. Their "health" (if one may call it that) is maintained with drugs, their weight is boosted with more drugs, and the result is your dinner! As chemicals tend to accrue in the organs, one should be sure that any organ meats come from organically raised animals.

For all this, meat IS a source of high-quality protein, and a tasty addition to the diet that few people are willing to give up. However, some changes in eating habits may be beneficial to our health as well as our purses. First, the Great-Big-Steak-or-Chop is out-dated and should be retired. We no longer work long, back-breaking hours clearing land, hauling water, chopping wood. Out of habit, we tend to eat more meat than we need. Second, there are many sources of protein other than meat that could assume more importance in our daily diet. We should eat smaller portions of meat, fewer meat meals.

Organic meats are available, but in small quantity, and not always in great variety. Laws pertaining to the slaughter and distribution of meat favour the large packing house. The original purpose of these laws was to protect the consumer from unclean meat, but their effect is to force the small farmer to sell his animals at large cattle auctions, rather than to individuals. This is unfortunate, as many small farmers *do* raise their animals organically. Not necessarily out of conviction, but simply because with a small, well-cared-for herd, all those tricky fattening routines would just be extra work. It may be possible to buy an animal "on the hoof," and have it taken to a custom processor. The cost shouldn't exceed retail, but you do need a large freezer!

As the demand for organically raised meats increases, the supply is increasing, but slowly. Meanwhile, trim all the fat possible from supermarket meats, and buy *lean* meats. Avoid organ meats and processed meats altogether unless you are sure they are free of adulterants such as nitrates, and are from organically raised animals. Health food stores do have some processed meats that are chemical-free.

The combination of fresh, pure meat with vegetables and herbs is a delicious one. There are many delectable ways to cook meats that are just as quick as steaks or chops, but use less meat per portion, and have much more flavour. Cool weather is a time when a savoury stew bubbling slowly can give the day a special kind of warmth, but we don't do all our cooking in cool weather, and we don't always have several hours to spend in the kitchen. We find the pressure cooker to be a great time-saver, as well as a conserver of fuel.

Katie's Stuffed Cabbage

1 *head cabbage, about 2 lbs.*

STUFFING MIXTURE

1 *lb. sausage meat (see page 137)**

2 *eggs, beaten*

$\frac{1}{3}$ *cup soy granules*

2 *oz. mild cheese, grated*

1 *cup cooked brown rice*

1$\frac{1}{2}$ *teaspoons salt*

dash pepper

$\frac{1}{2}$ *cup raisins*

2 *cups cooked or tinned tomatoes*

$\frac{1}{3}$ *cup wheat germ*

1 *small onion, minced*

1 *cup water*

*Ground beef may be used.

Separate the cabbage leaves gently. Drop them in boiling water just until the colour brightens. Drain and rinse with cold water.

Mix together the stuffing ingredients. Place 2 or 3 tablespoons of the stuffing in the centre of a cabbage leaf. Roll the stem end over to cover the stuffing, and fold the sides in toward the centre, then resume rolling. Continue until all the stuffing has been used. Reserve any leftover leaves.

Heat oven to 325°F.

Oil a large casserole and line it with the reserved leaves. Arrange the rolls in the casserole and add all of the remaining ingredients. Heat to boiling on top of the stove. (If your casserole is not up to that, heat the water, tomatoes, and onion and pour over the cabbage — add the wheat germ and raisins.)

Cover and bake 1$\frac{1}{2}$ hours, adding liquid if needed. *Serves 6.*

Pot Roast with Savory and Shallots

4–5 *lbs. silverside, preferably*
   with a bone
whole wheat flour
3 *tablespoons oil*
10 *shallots, minced*
1 *bunch summer savory*
   (approximately ¼ cup)
   minced

¾ *pint beef stock*
¼ *cup sherry*
1 *teaspoon salt*
dash pepper

Coat the roast with flour. Heat the oil in a pressure cooker (or Dutch oven). Brown the roast and stir in all the remaining ingredients, bring to a simmer and cook at 15 lbs. pressure for 35 minutes. (Or roast in Dutch oven about 2½ hours.) Thicken with flour and water mixed together, if needed. Correct seasoning.

Serves 6–8.

Easy Liver Bake

1 *lb. liver sliced about ½ inch*
   thick
½ *cup whole wheat flour*
1 *teaspoon paprika*
pinch thyme
1 *teaspoon salt*

2 *tablespoons wheat germ*
1 *large red or yellow onion,*
   sliced
2 *fl. oz. sherry*
6 *fl. oz. stock*

Oil a 9-inch ovenproof baking dish. Heat oven to 350°F.

Mix together the flour, paprika, thyme and salt. Dip the liver slices in the flour mixture and arrange them in the baking dish. Sprinkle with any remaining flour mixture and 1 tablespoon of the wheat germ. Top with the sliced onion. Mix the sherry with the stock and pour over the casserole. Top with the remaining 1 tablespoon wheat germ.

Bake at 350°F. for 30 minutes, or until the liver is done to taste.

Serves 4.

NOTE: Liver does not reheat very well.

Sautéed Liver

1 *lb. liver sliced about ½ inch*   2   *tablespoons   powdered*
  thick   *lecithin*
¼ *cup whole wheat flour*   2 *tablespoons oil*
¼ *cup wheat germ*

Mix together the flour, wheat germ and lecithin. Heat a large, heavy frying pan, and add the oil. Dip the liver slices in the flour mixture, and sauté them over medium heat for about 3 minutes on each side (med. rare) or to your taste. Sprinkle with salt and pepper.
  Serves 4.

Heart Rissoles

1 *beef heart (1½ to 2 pounds)*   3   *tablespoons   powdered*
3 *onions*   *lecithin*
1 *cup rolled oats*   *whole wheat flour*
2 *teaspoons salt*   *vegetable oil*
½ *teaspoon pepper*   1 *cup beef stock (optional)*

Remove excess fat and tendons from heart, and cut it into strips. Using a fine blade, mince the heart and the onions. Add the oats, salt, pepper and lecithin. Mix well and refrigerate the mixture overnight.
  Flour your hands and form rissoles, dipping them in flour.
  Heat the oil (enough to cover the bottom) in a large heavy frying pan. When the oil is hot, add the patties and cook over medium heat for about 5 minutes on each side, or until well browned. Remove to a heated platter.
  To make a gravy: If there is no oil in the pan, add enough to make about 2 tablespoons. Add about a tablespoon of the dipping flour. Stir to mix, and stir in the stock, carefully scraping up all the browned bits. Cook, stirring, to make a gravy. Season to taste.
  This recipe makes about 10 large rissoles.
NOTE: Heart Patties freeze well.

Baked Pork and Noodles

3½ lbs. lean pork, cubed

1 onion, finely chopped

1 cup finely chopped celery

1 teaspoon salt

½ teaspoon dried thyme

8 fl. oz. pork or chicken stock

1½ cups sliced mushrooms

1 cup cooked or frozen peas

2 tablespoons pimiento, diced

1 lb. uncooked wholewheat noodles

1 cup sour cream or yogurt

wheat germ

oil

Heat 2 tablespoons of the oil in a large frying pan. Brown the pork. Add the onion, celery, salt, thyme and stock. Cover and simmer 1 hour over low heat. (This may be done in advance. Reheat before continuing.)

Add the mushrooms, peas and pimiento to the pork mixture.

Oil a 4 pint casserole. Heat oven to 375°F.

Cook the noodles until just barely done, and drain them. Toss the drained noodles with the pork mixture, and fold in the sour cream or yogurt. Put it all into the prepared casserole and top with a generous sprinkling of wheat germ.

Bake at 375°F. for 30 minutes.

Serves 6.

Pork and Prune Casserole

1 lb lean pork, in ¼ inch slices

1 cup pitted prunes

salt and pepper to taste

2 tablespoons wheat germ

⅓ cup stock or water

juice of 1 lemon

¼ teaspoon thyme

1 large onion, sliced thinly

Arrange the pork in the casserole and sprinkle with 1 tablespoon of the wheat germ. Add the prunes and then the onion and thyme. Add the stock and lemon juice, and top with the remaining wheat germ. Bake for about 45 minutes, or until the pork is thoroughly done. Moisten with a little stock if needed.

Four rather small portions.

Barbara's Sausages

2 *lbs. minced pork*	$\frac{1}{2}$ *teaspoon thyme*
2 *teaspoons salt*	1 *teaspoon sage*
2 *tablespoons cider vinegar*	$1\frac{1}{2}$ *teaspoon pepper*
$\frac{1}{2}$ *teaspoon garlic powder*	$\frac{1}{2}$ *teaspoon allspice (powdered)*

Mix all ingredients very well. Stuff into sausage casings or form into rolls.

Sausages may be refrigerated for 3–4 days, or may be frozen for up to six months.

To Cook: Place rissoles or sausages in a heavy frying pan. Add about $\frac{1}{4}$ inch of water (don't cover the sausages). Heat the pan and its contents over medium heat until the sausages begin to change colour. Turn the sausages and cook for a few minutes more. Pour off the water carefully. Allow the sausages to cook until they are brown on one side, and then turn them and brown the other side.

Savoury Pork and Apple Stew

$1\frac{1}{2}$ *lbs. lean pork, diced into* 1″ *cubes*	$\frac{1}{4}$ *teaspoon cinnamon*
	$\frac{3}{4}$ *pint stock or water*
2 *tablespoons oil*	$\frac{1}{4}$ *teaspoon dried sage*
2 *med. onions, in chunks*	*salt and pepper to taste*
2 *cups diced sweet potato*	2 *cooking apples, cored and diced*
1 *leafy stalk celery, diced*	

Heat the oil in a large, heavy pan. Brown the pork. Stir in the onions, sweet potato, celery, cinnamon and water. Cover and simmer 45 minutes.

Add the sage, salt and pepper, and the apples, simmer 15 minutes more. Thicken with flour and water paste, if desired.

Serves 4.

Stuffed Peppers

We make the filling first, then pick the peppers. The number of peppers depends on the size available. As the recipe is to serve six, you might start with six large peppers, with one or two smaller ones for any leftover stuffing. There is no reason you can't use a dozen or so small peppers if that is what you have.

Sweet peppers, as ripe and red as possible. See note above. Cut a thin slice from the stem end and remove the seeds
4 oz. raw brown rice
12 fl. oz. vegetable cooking water, stock or plain water
2 tablespoons vegetable oil
1 medium onion, chopped
1 lb. minced beef, lamb or pork
1 clove garlic

1 teaspoon salt
2 ripe tomatoes, peeled and chopped
½ cup wheat germ
2 tablespoons lemon juice
½ teaspoon powdered ginger
2 tablespoons finely chopped parsley
2 eggs, beaten
4 fl. oz. stock, cooking water or water

Add the rice to the cooking water. Bring to a boil. Cover, lower heat and simmer 20 minutes.

Meanwhile, heat the oil and sauté the onion and meat until done. Add the garlic, crushed.

Mix the meat mixture with the rice, salt, tomatoes, wheat germ, lemon juice, parsley and eggs.

Stuff the peppers with the rice-meat mixture. Place the peppers, stuffed end up in a large, heavy pot. Add the stock, bring to a boil, cover and simmer 30 minutes. Don't let the pot boil dry.

Serves 6.

Bulghur Meat Loaf

¾ cup bulghur
1½ lbs. mince

1 medium onion, chopped
1 tablespoon peanut oil

2 *teaspoons salt*   1 *cup yogurt*
2 *eggs, lightly beaten*   3 *tablespoons soy flour*

Soak the bulghur in water to cover for ½ hour. Drain.

Heat the oil and sauté the onion until it is barely transparent.

Heat oven to 325°F.

Place the meat in a very large bowl. Add everything else and mix thoroughly using two forks. (The fork-mixing is the secret of good texture in meat loaves.) With the forks, place the meat mixture in a loaf pan. Press gently with the fork to remove any air spaces.

Bake at 325°F. about 1 hour or until interior temperature is 180°F. on a meat thermometer.

Short Ribs of Beef
Economical and tasty

4 *lbs. short ribs of beef*   1 *clove (optional)*
3 *medium onions, cut up*   *few sprigs parsley*
2 *carrots, cut up*   1 *sprig thyme (½ teaspoon*
2 *tablespoons whole wheat*   *dried)*
  flour   *salt and pepper to taste*
1 *cup red wine*   *beef stock or water*
1 *bay leaf*

In a large pressure cooker (or dutch oven), brown the ribs in their own fat, a few at a time. Pour off all but about 3 tablespoons fat and add the onions and carrots. Stir until the onion is becoming translucent, then add the flour. Mix well, then add the wine, taking care to stir all of the browned bits from the bottom of the pan. Tie the bay leaf, clove, parsley and thyme into a little cheesecloth bag and add them to the pot. Add the salt and pepper and enough water or stock to cover the ribs by one-third. Bring the liquid to a full boil, cover and cook at 15 lbs. pressure for 15 minutes (or simmer, covered, for about 2 hours.) Remove the cheesecloth bag and discard.

Serves 4.

This dish is best made a day or two in advance, as short ribs tend to be fatty, and the chilled fat is easily removed. The sauce may be thickened with flour and water paste, if desired.

*⅓ of the meat should be above water.

Basic Beef Stew

2 lbs. stewing beef in 1½ inch cubes
whole wheat flour
3 tablespoons oil
2 medium onions, chopped
1 carrot, cut up
2 pints stock
⅓ pint red wine (or another ⅓ pint of stock)
few sprigs parsley
sprig thyme
1 bay leaf
1 clove garlic, crushed
salt and pepper to taste
6 medium potatoes, diced
6 carrots, cut in chunks
6 medium onions, in chunks
2 peppers, in chunks

Roll the beef cubes in seasoned flour to coat.

Heat the oil. Brown the floured cubes in the oil, a few at a time. Add the 2 onions and the 1 carrot. Stir in the stock and wine, stirring up all the browned bits from the bottom of the pot. Tie the parsley, thyme and bay leaf together and add to the pot. (Dried herbs may be tied in a little cheesecloth bag.) Add the garlic, salt and pepper. Bring to a boil, lower the heat, cover and simmer 1½ hours.

Add the potatoes and remaining carrots. Cover and simmer 25 minutes.

Add the remaining onions and the peppers. Cover and simmer 10 minutes. Remove the herbs.

Thicken if desired with flour and water paste.

Other vegetables may be added or substituted.

Serves 6.

Ham Loaf

2 *lbs. minced ham*
$\frac{1}{4}$ *cup fresh whole wheat bread crumbs*
$\frac{1}{4}$ *cup wheat germ*
$\frac{1}{2}$ *green pepper, chopped*
1 *teaspoon prepared mustard*

$\frac{1}{4}$ *teaspoon thyme*
$\frac{1}{4}$ *teaspoon minced parsley*
2 *eggs*
$\frac{1}{2}$ *cup milk*
salt to taste

Heat oven to 350°F.

Combine all ingredients, pack into a loaf pan, and bake for one hour. Serve hot or cold.

Marinated Shish-Kebabs

2 *lbs. beef fillet cut in* 1″ *cubes*
1 *tablespoon salt*
$\frac{1}{2}$ *teaspoon freshly ground black pepper*
$\frac{1}{2}$ *teaspoon oregano*
$\frac{1}{2}$ *teaspoon lemon juice*
1 *green pepper, seeded and cut in chunks*

several cherry tomatoes or large tomatoes, cut up
pearl onions or large onions, cut up
several mushrooms, quartered
oil
lemon wedges

Place the meat, salt, pepper and oregano in a glass container, cover with oil and allow to marinate in the refrigerator overnight.

When you are ready to cook the kebabs, drain the meat, and thread it on skewers, alternating with green pepper, tomatoes, onion and mushrooms. Sprinkle with the lemon juice and grill or barbecue until done to taste.

Serve hot with lemon wedges.

Serves 6.

Slow Swiss Steak

2 *lbs. braising steak*	2 *cups tinned tomatoes, chopped*
2 *tablespoons whole wheat flour*	1 *large onion, sliced*
1 *teaspoon salt*	1 *stalk celery, sliced*
$\frac{1}{4}$ *teaspoon pepper*	1 *clove garlic, crushed*
2 *tablespoons vegetable oil*	1 *teaspoon Worcestershire sauce*

The steak should be sliced into serving sized pieces about $\frac{1}{2}$ inch thick. Pound the pieces to about $\frac{1}{4}$ inch thick and dust with flour, salt and pepper. Heat the oil in a frying pan and brown the steaks lightly.

Place the browned steaks with all the remaining ingredients in slow cooker. Cover and cook over LOW heat for 6 to 8 hours.

Serve with cooked brown rice or potatoes.
Serves 4.

Bran Meat Loaf
(Inexpensive and delicious)

$\frac{1}{2}$ *lb. minced beef*	2 *teaspoons Worcestershire sauce*
1 *cup bran flakes*	$\frac{1}{2}$ *teaspoon pepper*
1 *cup cottage cheese*	1 *teaspoon salt*
2 *eggs*	$\frac{1}{2}$ *cup soy granules*
2 *tablespoons tomato paste*	8 *fl. oz. tomato juice*
$\frac{1}{2}$ *teaspoon thyme*	

Heat oven to 350°F.

In a large bowl, mix all the ingredients in order. Use a fork to mix. Place the mixture gently into the pan and smooth the top with the fork. Bake for about one hour or until done through.

Lamb Shanks with Lentils

1 *lamb shank per person*	½ *teaspoon rosemary*
garlic	*dash cayenne*
3 *tablespoons oil*	1 *lb. dried lentils*
1 *onion, minced*	¼ *cup chopped parsley*
2¾ *cups stock*	4 *spring onions, chopped finely*
¼ *cup lemon juice*	

Heat oven to 350°F. Slice the garlic into slivers and insert the slivers into the shanks. Brown the shanks in 2 tablespoons oil and then roast the shanks on a rack in the preheated oven for one hour. Place a pan beneath the rack to catch the drippings.

Sauté the onion in 1 tablespoon oil until translucent. Add the stock, lemon juice, rosemary and cayenne and bring to a boil. Add the lentils. Return to a boil, cover and simmer ½ hour. Stir the parsley and spring onions into the cooked lentils along with 2 tablespoons of the lamb drippings. Top with the lamb shanks and serve.

Stuffed Savoy Cabbage

1 *large Savoy cabbage*	¼ *teaspoon basil*
1 *lb. minced beef*	*salt and pepper to taste*
1 *large onion, chopped*	2 *tablespoons oil*
1 *clove garlic, crushed*	2 *large carrots, sliced*
4 *teaspoons tomato paste*	1 *large onion, sliced*
½ *cup cooked brown rice*	3 *cups meat stock (water may*
1 *egg*	*be used)*
½ *teaspoon thyme*	

Drop the whole cabbage into boiling salted water to cover for 10 to 15 minutes. Drain and rinse with cold water. Allow to cool. Remove very tough or discoloured outer leaves.

Place cabbage, stem side down on a large square of cheesecloth. Gently pry the leaves apart and cut out the core, leaving the stem intact. Mix together the meat, chopped onion, garlic, tomato paste, rice, egg, thyme, basil, salt and pepper. Place the mixture into the hollow cabbage and gently reshape the leaves, re-forming the cabbage. Tie the cheesecloth around the cabbage firmly.

Heat the oil in a large pan. Sauté the carrots and sliced onion very briefly and add the cabbage and stock. Cover and cook at simmer for $2\frac{1}{2}$–3 hours. Remove the cheesecloth before serving.

Serves 4.

Oven "Fried" Chicken
Crispy and delicious!

2 *small roasting chickens, about $2\frac{1}{2}$ lbs. each**	1 *oz. wheat germ*
	2 *teaspoons medium paprika*
1 *egg*	1 *teaspoon garlic powder*
$\frac{1}{3}$ *cup yogurt*	2 *teaspoons salt*
4 *oz. whole wheat flour*	$\frac{1}{2}$ *teaspoon pepper*

* Small birds should be quartered. Larger birds may be used, but should be disjointed.

Beat the egg with the yogurt. Mix the flour with the wheat germ, paprika, garlic, salt and pepper.

Heat the oven to 350°F. Oil a large baking sheet.

One at a time, dip the chicken pieces into the egg-yogurt mixture, then into the flour mixture. Place the coated pieces on the baking sheet, without allowing them to touch.

Bake the chicken at 350°F., turning the pieces at 15 minute intervals. Small chickens will take *about* 40 minutes, larger chickens will take *about* 50.

Serves 4.

Simple Boiled Chicken

1 *stewing hen, 4–5 lbs.*
1 *medium onion, peeled and chunked*
2 *cloves garlic*
2 *carrots, in chunks*
1 *bay leaf*

1 *teaspoon salt*
1 *leafy stalk celery*
few sprigs parsley
pinch thyme
4 *pints water*

Wash the hen thoroughly and put it in a very large pot with all of the other ingredients. Bring the water to a boil, cover the pot and simmer at very low heat for 1½ hours or until the chicken is tender.

The chicken may be eaten as it is, and the stock makes an excellent soup, or use some of the chicken for salad or **chicken cream**.

Chicken Cream

2–3 *cups diced cooked chicken*
1 *cup chopped broccoli*
1 *carrot, sliced*
1 *medium onion, in chunks*
¼ *pint chicken stock*
1 *oz. butter*

2 *tablespoons oil*
1 *cup sliced mushrooms*
1 *oz. whole wheat flour*
8 *fl. oz. chicken stock*
8 *fl. oz. milk*

Simmer the broccoli, carrot and onion in the ¼ pint chicken stock for 10 minutes. Set aside.

Heat the butter and oil together and stir in the mushrooms, cook 2–3 minutes over low heat. Stir in the wheat flour. Cook 2–3 minutes and add the stock, stirring constantly, then add the milk and cook the mixture over low heat, stirring, for about 10 minutes or until the sauce is thick. Add the chicken. Drain the vegetables and add them. If the sauce is too thick, add some of the vegetable cooking stock. Taste for seasoning.

Serve over rice or noodles.

Serves 4–6.

Roast Turkey
Definitely un-stuffy

12 *lb. turkey (will serve eight,*   1–2 *sprigs parsley*
   generously)   1–2 *sprigs sage*
1 *celery stalk with leaves*   *salt*
1 *onion*

Heat oven to 325°F. Place oiled meat rack in large baking dish. Remove giblets and neck from turkey. Cut off wing tips if you wish. Wash turkey inside and out with cool water. Dry. Sprinkle cavity lightly with salt. Place onion, celery, parsley and sage in cavity.

Place turkey on rack and roast at 325°F. 4 to 4½ hours or until meat thermometer in thigh registers 180°F., or juices run clear. Remove turkey to warm platter. Save pan juices for gravy.

NOTE: If the turkey seems to be browning too fast, cover it with cheesecloth dipped in oil or melted butter. Remove the cloth for the last few minutes of roasting.

Giblet Stock

Neck, giblets and maybe wing-   1 *bay leaf*
   tips from your turkey   *pinch salt*
1 *leafy celery stalk*   *dash pepper*
1 *carrot*   4 *pints water*
1 *onion*

Put everything into pot. Bring to a boil, skim, lower heat and simmer for 1½ hours. Strain broth. Save neck and giblets. Discard bay leaf and vegetables.

Un-Stuffing
You don't need a bird to make it

4 *tablespoons oil*
8 *cups, soft, fresh, whole wheat bread torn into small cubes*
1 *sweet red pepper, chopped*
1 *sweet green pepper, chopped*
1 *medium onion, chopped*

1 *stalk celery, chopped*
1–2 *sprigs sage, minced ($\frac{1}{2}$ teaspoon dried, powdered sage)*
salt and pepper to taste
giblet stock

Heat oil and sauté vegetables until soft. Add bread and stir until bread is lightly toasted. Toss in sage and mix well. Add salt and pepper to taste.

Oil a 5-pint casserole. Fill with stuffing. Add one-half to one cup or more giblet stock, depending on how moist you like your stuffing.

Cover casserole and bake at 325°F. for about 20 minutes. Remove cover and let bake another 20 minutes or until crusty around edges.

Un-Stuffing may be made ahead and re-heated, covered, in the oven.

Fancy Un-Stuffing

Add to the un-stuffing whatever you like best: diced giblets, oysters, chestnuts, walnuts, mushrooms, diced apples. Make more than one kind of un-stuffing!

Turkey Hash

3 tablespoons oil
1 medium onion, chopped finely
2 cloves garlic, chopped finely
2 tablespoons whole wheat flour
1½ cups stock or vegetable cooking water

¼ cup yogurt
2 cups diced cooked turkey
½ cup chopped, pitted black olives
2 hard-boiled eggs, chopped
1 teaspoon minced fresh basil
1 teaspoon salt
pepper to taste

Heat oil and sauté onion and garlic until onion is translucent. Stir in flour. Add stock a little at a time and cook until thickened. Stir in everything else and cook just to heat through. Serve with noodles or whole wheat scones.
Serves 4.

Turkey Gravy

pan drippings from a roast turkey
3–4 tablespoons whole wheat flour

1–1½ pints boiling giblet stock
salt to taste

The amount of flour you need depends upon the amount of fat in the drippings. It is fairly easy to estimate if you stir in the flour one tablespoon at a time. When all the fat is mixed thickly with flour, there is enough flour.

Place the roasting pan on the stove over very low heat. Add the flour one tablespoon at a time until all the fat is absorbed. Use more or less flour as you need it. Scrape up all the browned bits. Stir in the boiling stock a little at a time, let cook to thicken. Add salt to taste.

If the gravy is too thick, thin it with giblet stock. To thicken, add one tablespoon cornflour, mixed with two tablespoons water.

Giblet Gravy

Add cooked diced giblets to the completed gravy.

Whole Grains and Pasta

If your grocer offered you pale green or yellow spinach, claiming that it was "just as good," but the vitamin A was removed to improve the spinach's keeping qualities, would you buy it? Not likely; yet we spend millions of pounds every year on flour, rice, wheat, noodles, etc., from which many of the nutrients have been removed in the interests of "shelf-life." Nothing is "improved" by having vital nutrients removed. There is something awry when whole brown rice costs MORE than the polished white rice which has consumed many more man and machine hours in the processing. If whole grains were stored properly, that is, refrigerated, it might explain some part of their premium price. Most supermarkets, however, stick them on the shelves with their de-vitalized cousins, where the natural oils are subject to becoming rancid.

Whole grains contain a germ which is the living seed from which new sprouts grow. The germ contains Vitamin E, as well as valuable protein. The bran, or outer coating of the grain, contains vitamins and minerals.

As protein, whole grains make a valuable contribution to the diet. Kasha (buckwheat groats) is about 12% protein, bulghur about 10%, and brown rice about 7½% when measured dry. "Enriched" white rice is reduced to 6.7% protein. Whole grains are a source of B vitamins, calcium, phosphorous, and lecithin. They also taste far better than their pale, de-natured counterparts, demonstrating again that the food that is best nutritionally is usually the best tasting, too.

Homemade Bulghur

1 cup of whole wheat = 1 cup of bulghur

Wash the wheat well and put it in a pot with water to just barely cover the wheat. Bring it to a boil and cook covered over low heat until all the water has been absorbed — about one half-hour. Spread the wheat on a baking sheet and dry in a low oven — 200°F. for about one hour or until dry. You may be able to dry it over direct heat, stirring to prevent scorching. The bulghur should be cracked into coarse pieces.

Bulghur Pilaff

2 *tablespoons peanut or sun-*   2 *cups stock or vegetable cook-*
   flower oil   *ing water*
1 *onion, chopped finely*   1 *teaspoon salt – if needed*
1 *cup bulghur*

Heat the oil in a heavy pot. Add the onions and cook until the onions are becoming transparent. Add the bulghur and stir to coat the grains with the oil. Add the stock. Whether or not you need salt and how much will depend on whether the stock is seasoned. If you want to add salt, add it now. Bring the mixture to a boil. Cover the pot, lower the heat and let the bulghur simmer until all the liquid has been absorbed — about 15 minutes.

You can add nuts to the cooked pilaff. You can also make it with mushrooms. Chop the mushrooms and add them at the same time as the onions. You might like to try adding your favourite herbs, too. Pilaff is a dish that should allow your imagination to run free!

Tabbouleh — Bulghur Salad

Bulghur can be used as a salad. This recipe is a classic but there are many variations possible.

½ *cup bulghur*
1 *small onion, chopped finely*
1 *spring onion, chopped finely*
½ *cup chopped fresh parsley (¼ cup dried)*

⅓ *cup lemon juice*
3 *tablespoons mint leaves, chopped (3 teaspoons dried)*
¼ *cup olive oil*
3 *or 4 tomatoes, cut in wedges*

Soak the bulghur in cold water to cover for 30 minutes. Drain, place the bulghur on a cloth and wring out the excess water.

Mix the onion, spring onion, parsley and lemon juice. Toss with the bulghur. Refrigerate at least ½ hour.

Meanwhile, add the mint to the olive oil. Mix with the bulghur mixture just before serving.

To serve, mound the bulghur on a plate and garnish with the tomato wedges. The tomatoes can be chopped fine and added to the bulghur mixture.

Serves 4.

Bulghur Breakfast Cereal

1 *cup bulghur*
2½ *cups water*
½ *cup raisins*

Heat the water and bulghur to boiling. Cook over low heat, stirring occasionally until it is thick and the water has all been absorbed; about 15 minutes. Turn off the heat and stir in the raisins. Let stand two to three minutes to plump the raisins. Serve hot.

Creamy Bulghur & Cheese Casserole

2 *tablespoons oil*
1 *medium onion, chopped*
1 *clove garlic, minced*
2 *cups water*
salt and pepper to taste
1 *large, ripe tomato, peeled and sliced thinly*

1 *cup cottage cheese*
1 *egg beaten with ½ cup water*
2 *tablespoons freshly chopped parsley*
cheddar cheese

Heat the oil and gently sauté the onion and garlic until the onion is translucent. Add the bulghur and stir for about 2 minutes. Add the water, bring to a boil, cover and simmer for 30 minutes.

While the bulghur is cooking, heat the oven to 350°F. and oil a 5 pint casserole.

Place about two-thirds of the cooked bulghur in a layer in the bottom of the casserole. Sprinkle with salt and pepper to taste. Add the sliced tomato in a layer. Mix the cottage cheese with the egg and ½ cup water. Stir in the parsley and add salt and pepper to taste. Pour the cottage cheese mixture over the tomatoes and top with the remaining bulghur. Garnish with a thin layer of sliced or grated cheddar cheese. Bake 30 minutes.

Serves 4.

Kasha

A great change from potatoes, rice, noodles, etc.

1 *egg*
1 *cup kasha (buckwheat groats)*
2 *cups boiling water*

2 *tablespoons oil*
1 *medium onion, finely chopped*
salt and pepper to taste

Mix the egg with the kasha in a heavy pot (*not* enamelled), stir the kasha mixture until dry. Add the boiling water and cook the kasha over gentle heat until the water has all been absorbed. The kasha should be just tender. You may add

a little more water if it is needed. Keep the kasha warm.
Heat the oil and sauté the onion until it is translucent. Toss the oil and onion with the kasha. Season to taste.
Serves 4.

Bulghur stuffing for Poultry or Vegetables

$\frac{3}{4}$ *cup bulghur*
1 *medium onion*
1 *stalk celery*
2 *tablespoons peanut oil*
1 *clove garlic*
$\frac{1}{2}$ *teaspoon dried sage*
$\frac{1}{4}$ *teaspoon thyme (dried, whole)*

$\frac{1}{2}$ *teaspoon sweet paprika*
2 *teaspoons salt*
$\frac{1}{2}$ *cup chopped parsley ($\frac{1}{4}$ cup dried)*
$\frac{1}{4}$ *pint chicken stock*
1 *oz. sunflower seeds*

Soak the bulghur in water to cover for half-an-hour. Chop the onion and celery finely.

Heat the peanut oil in a large frying pan. Add the onion and celery and stir until the celery begins to turn brighter. Drain the bulghur and add it to the pan. Stir to coat with oil. Add the garlic, squished through a press. Add everything else and stir over low heat until all the liquid has been absorbed. Let cool.

This is enough stuffing for a large chicken. Any leftover stuffing mix can be cooked with more stock and served as a side dish. Just keep adding stock, a little at a time, until the bulghur is as soft as you like.

Chinese Fried Rice

2 *tablespoons peanut oil*
1 *teaspoon salt*
1 *medium onion, finely diced*
1 *stalk celery, finely diced*
½ *cup cooked meat, poultry or prawns, diced (optional)*
2 *eggs, lightly beaten*

½ *cup fresh or frozen peas*
1 *cup bean sprouts*
6 *cups cold, cooked brown rice*
3 *tablespoons soy sauce (or to taste)*
green part of two spring onions, chopped finely

Heat the peanut oil in a wok or very large frying pan. Add the salt, onion, celery and meat and stir until the onion is becoming translucent. Mix in the eggs, stirring. As soon as they are set, add the peas and bean sprouts and mix well. Add the rice and the soy sauce and mix thoroughly. Taste for seasoning. The rice does not really fry at all, it should only be heated through. Garnish with the chopped spring onions.
   Serves 6.

Basic Rice

Generally you will want about 3 oz. of uncooked rice per person. Place the brown rice in a heavy pot. You should not need to wash it. Shake the pot to make the surface of the rice even and smooth. Rest a forefinger on top of the rice, so gently that it does not make a dent. Add cold water to the depth of your first knuckle (roughly 1 inch). Set the pan over high heat and bring to a boil. Cover the pan and lower the heat. Cook over low heat for about 20 minutes or until the rice is fat and fluffy and small holes appear on the surface. Rice is properly kept warm over lowest possible heat until it is served.

Jewelled Rice Pilaff

2 *tablespoons oil*
⅓ *cup chopped onion*

1 *oz. sunflower seeds*
6 *oz. brown rice*

⅓ cup chopped apricots

2 oz. currants or chopped raisins

1¼ pints boiling water

salt and pepper to taste

Heat the oil in a large pot and sauté the onion until soft. Add the sunflower seeds and rice and cook about 2 minutes more, stirring. Stir in the apricots and currants. Add the boiling water and return to the boil. Cover and simmer 40 minutes or until the rice is done. Season to taste with salt and pepper.

Serves 6.

Seven-grain Breakfast Bowl

4½ cups water

¼ cup whole oats

¼ cup barley

¼ cup wheat flakes

¼ cup buckwheat groats (kasha)

¼ cup brown rice

2 tablespoons rye grains

2 tablespoons millet

¼ teaspoon salt

Heat water to boiling and stir in the grains and salt. Return to the boil, cover, lower heat to simmer and cook for about 90 minutes, stirring occasionally.

Serves 4–6.

Homemade Pasta

Home pasta-making is enjoying a revival. Pasta machines are abundant in kitchen shops and gift catalogues. As with other foods, store-bought pasta just can't be compared to homemade, especially when your pasta is made with hearty, chewy whole wheat flour. Pasta-making can be compared to bread-making. Both are time-consuming, both require kneading, and both can offer a constructive way to get rid of tensions. Problems can be mixed and kneaded and rolled and chopped into oblivion. Pasta dough is tough and not too elastic, and requires fairly rough handling in the initial stages of rolling the dough.

One of the special pleasures of pasta-making is the variety of shapes and sizes and uses to which pasta lends itself. You may cut long thin noodles, short thin noodles, short fat noodles, triangles, diamonds, squares — virtually anything. You can serve pasta in soup, top it with a sauce, stuff it, bake it, boil it, or just serve it all by itself with a little butter.

An interesting variation on the theme of pasta is the Hungarian tarhonya. Tarhonya is simply chopped and dried pasta cooked as a side dish or accompaniment. It is spectacular with a fine goulash, naturally, but goes well with just about any main dish, especially if there is a little sauce or gravy.

Working with pasta requires a bit of common sense. Essentially, the dough is simply a combination of flour and egg. Eggs will vary in size, and flour will vary in the amount of moisture it can absorb. If you mix your ingredients as directed and the dough is too soft, knead it on a well-floured surface until it is no longer sticky. If, on the other hand, the dough is too hard, dampen your hands (just *damp*— not dripping wet) and knead the dough until the water is absorbed. If the dough is still too stiff, repeat the process until the dough is of the right consistency.

Fresh pasta may be stored in an airtight container in the refrigerator for several days. It may also be frozen, but frozen pasta must be cooked without thawing.

Whole Wheat Noodles

4 oz. whole wheat flour
dash salt
1 whole egg
1 egg yolk
1 teaspoon vegetable oil

Mix together the salt, egg, egg yolk and vegetable oil. Make a well in the centre of the flour and add the egg mixture. Stir gently with a fork to incorporate the egg mixture, then mix with your hands and knead about 10 minutes, or until the dough is smooth and elastic. Divide the dough into two portions.

Working with one portion at a time, pat the dough into a ball, then flatten it slightly. On a lightly floured surface, roll the dough as thinly as possible. Flour the dough lightly and wrap it around the rolling pin. Roll the dough-wrapped pin back and forth until the dough is very thin. Gently unwrap the dough from the rolling pin, let it dry for 10 minutes and fold it accordian-style. With a sharp knife, cut the dough into shreds of whatever width you desire. Pick up the noodles and hang over a towel rack or the back of a wooden chair for about 10 minutes. Repeat with remaining dough. Use the noodles immediately, or wrap tightly and refrigerate for 2–3 days.

Makes 2 servings. Recipe may be doubled.

NOTE: If using a pasta machine for rolling and cutting — follow manufacturer's instructions.

Tarhonya

1 *lb. whole wheat flour*
1 *teaspoon salt*
3 *eggs*

Make a well in the centre of the flour and stir in the eggs and salt. Knead to make a smooth, elastic dough. Roll the dough as thin as possible, and cut into ⅛ inch strips. Chop strips until the bits of dough are as fine as barley. Spread on baking sheets and dry in 150°F. oven for about 1 hour. Store in a tightly covered container.

TO COOK:
1 *medium onion, chopped*
2 *tablespoons vegetable oil*
1 *cup tarhonya*
3 *cups stock or water*

Heat the oil and sauté the onion until golden. Add the tarhonya and stir to coat with oil. Add the stock, bring to a boil, and simmer until all the stock is absorbed (about 20 minutes). Season to taste.
Serves 4.

Basic Green Noodles

14 *oz. whole wheat flour*   1½ *cups chopped, cooked spi-*
2 *eggs, lightly beaten*   *nach, drained*

Put the flour on a pastry board or into a very large bowl. Make a well in the centre of the flour and carefully pour in the eggs. With your hands or a towel, squeeze as much liquid as possible from the spinach. Add ¾ cup of the dry spinach to the flour and eggs. Knead all the ingredients together for about 15 minutes until the dough is smooth and elastic. Dampen your hands if the dough seems dry.
  Divide the dough into 3 or 4 sections and roll out one section at a time on a well-floured pastry board. Cut the

dough with a sharp knife to make whatever size and shape of noodle you wish, or roll and cut with a pasta machine following manufacturer's directions.

Cook the noodles in boiling salted water until cooked to taste.

Uncooked noodles may be frozen and cooked as above without thawing.

Serves 4–6.

Noodles with Poppy Seeds

8 *oz. of your favourite broad*   3 *oz. almonds, chopped*
   noodles, cooked and hot   2 *tablespoons oil*
2 *tablespoons poppy seeds*

Mix the poppy seeds with the almonds. Heat the oil and briefly toast the seed and nut mixture. Toss the hot mixture with the hot noodles.

Serves 6.

Honest Bread

Bread is an ancient food. The Egyptians built ovens in which to bake leavened bread. The Chinese have made bread for thousands of years, although theirs is steamed rather than baked. The American pioneers had their bread, too. In fact, the supplies recommended to travellers crossing the prairies were limited to flour, bacon, coffee, sugar, yeast, salt, pepper and beef on the hoof. Citric acid was advised for folks travelling where fresh vegetables or fruit were not available. Fortunately for America, rolling mills which produced white, refined flour were invented in 1834 and since "civilization" travelled slowly in those days, most of the pioneers carried stoneground whole wheat flour.

Your great-grandmother may have been no great cook but hers was an honest loaf of bread. We have lost touch with many of the good things of the earth and in doing so, we have lost touch with something in ourselves. We need that touch of earth, our connection with our heritage. In our searching for that somewhat mystical connection, we find a growing taste for honest bread; dark, moist and warm from the oven.

There is nothing very sustaining about a loaf of white bread, wrapped in plastic, uniformly sliced and possessed of an unreal texture and eerily tasteless "flavour." There is more variation in the flavour of tap water than in those identical loaves of white bread. Is this the "staff of life?" Emphatically not! Real, honest bread is a thing of beauty. Dark, rich, crumbly, with a distinctive flavour and aroma. I t is a nourishing, soul-satisfying food. It's just possible that the American and British addiction to the sandwich is more of an attempt to bring some sort of hearty flavour to plastic white bread, rather than simply a search for "quick food." Most of the homemade, wholewheat bread fans we know take their bread "straight" or with a little honey or nut butter. Add a salad or soup or cheese or yogurt or a hard boiled egg and — PRESTO! — lunch!

In nutritional terms, white bread, even though it is "enriched" and made with 2 percent non-fat dry milk, does not compare favourably with whole wheat bread. Our figures are based on the United States government Handbook No. 8, *Composition of Foods*. For their sample, they used shop bought breads, made with all the dough conditioners, spoilage retardents, etc. Therefore, the figures for both white and whole wheat bread reflect the sodium and calcium content of these additives. The whole wheat bread has about 15 percent more calcium and slightly more sodium but 33 percent more sodium propionate is added to the dough! Whole wheat bread has 25 percent more protein than white bread, 200 percent more phosphorous, almost 300 percent more potassium, about 300 percent more magnesium and is about equal to "enriched" bread in iron, thiamine, riboflavin and niacin.

Making homemade yeast bread is a little like making pottery, all the words in the world are no substitute for putting your hands in and trying it yourself. Dough is alive. It has a texture and tone that can only be appreciated by touching, poking and kneading. Words will tell you to knead the dough until it's smooth and elastic but only your hands and eyes will tell you when that occurs.

For step-by-step directions on how to knead dough, see steps 5 through 10 of the High Protein Whole Wheat Bread recipe, page 167.

Before you start, it is helpful to have some understanding of the ingredients that go into bread and how they work. Once the ingredients have been mixed, it's too late to change anything. Everything has to be right at the beginning. Fortunately, breadmaking is more of an art than a science. As in pottery making, you will soon begin to "feel" when your dough is right. Once you have mastered the simple basic process, you can dream up all sorts of exciting variations. Knowing what is happening and why is the key to successful breadmaking.

Yeast is a living organism which feeds on the sugars in the dough and produces bubbles that make it rise. Yeast may be purchased in compressed cakes, small packages of dried yeast or bulk packages, also dried. The bulk packages are found at health food stores and are the most economical and usually the freshest. Yeast should be stored in the refrigerator. When it is used, it should be added to liquid which is at a temperature of 110° to 115°. All other ingredients should be at room temperature.

$\frac{1}{2}$ **ounce dry yeast = 1 package =1 cake.**

Sugar is what yeast lives on. Happily, yeast can't tell sugar from honey or molasses.

Salt slows down the bubbling action of the yeast, lengthens the rising time to allow the flour to develop.

Flour is the main ingredient in bread. Wheat flour contains gluten, a protein that stretches to support the bubbles formed by the yeast, making the bread light. Different types of wheat have different amounts of gluten. The high-gluten flours are usually sold as bread flour, while the lower gluten flours are labelled pastry flour. Whole wheat flours are proportionately lower in gluten than white flours, consequently, whole wheat breads are heavier and denser than white breads. If you want lighter bread, replace *some* of the whole wheat flour with unbleached flour but you will be sacrificing nutrition for appearance! Wheat flour naturally tastes best when it's fresh, so buy it from a dealer who has a fairly rapid turnover (your health food dealer) and who keeps it cool (ditto).

Flours vary tremendously in their capacity to absorb moisture. Some of the factors influencing the absorbtive qualities of flour are humidity in the air, age of the flour, milling of the flour, humidity of the place where it was stored, etc. You have to use your eyes and hands to judge exactly how much flour you need. Flour should be added slowly, until the desired consistency is achieved. You can always add more flour if you need it; you can't remove it if you add too much!

Fat may be butter, lard or oil. It helps with the elasticity of the dough and makes the bread tender.

Liquid. Bread may be made with milk, vegetable cooking water, beer, or simply water. Honey, molasses and eggs must be considered part of the liquid measurement. **NOTE:** Raw milk *must* be scalded or it will make your bread gummy.

Eggs add protein and improve the structure of some breads.

Other Ingredients. We add soy flour for protein, dry milk for protein and calcium, wheat germ for flavour and Vitamin E, caraway seeds or sesame seeds or herbs for flavour, etc. Any of these additions are optional. They do tend to make the bread a bit heavier but we enjoy the range of experimentation such additions allow. Powdered ingredients must be subtracted from the total flour content. Thus, if your bread called for 2 lbs. flour and you added 2 oz. of wheat germ and 2 oz. of soy flour, you would reduce your wheat flour to 1 lb. 12 oz. Dried herbs should be added during the first mixing but seeds, fresh herbs, dried fruits, nuts, etc. may be kneaded in after the first rise.

Powdered Ginger. A friend who makes a living teaching breadmaking uses a pinch of powdered ginger to "annoy" the yeast and provoke it to a frenzy of bubbly activity. We have used it successfully.

Lard. Oil your breadpans if you must but if you have clean, chemical-free lard, grease your breadpans with it. It is the best anti-sticking agent for wheat bread. Liquid lecithin is also excellent.

Utensils. Good bread deserves its own kneading board. Any large hardwood board will do, but it should not be used for cutting meat or poultry. Bread can be kneaded on a super-clean counter or table. We bought a large breadboard from a restaurant supply house.

A thermometer that measures as low as 105°F. is useful for testing the temperature at which yeast lives. Dairy thermometers measure in this range, as well as some kitchen thermometers.

Unless you intend to make bread in one-loaf batches, you will need a large bowl. Our 8-pint bowl is just barely adequate.

Bread can be baked in anything. If you don't have any bread pans, make round loaves or baguettes and bake them on a baking sheet. Bread pans don't have to be fancy, just loaf-shaped. If you are new to cooking with whole grains and honey, you might find an oven-proof glass pan useful, as you can see how brown the bottom of the loaf is getting.

Setting Dough to Rise. A gas oven with a pilot light is an ideal place but any place that is warm, draught-free and about 80°–90°F. will do. With cooler homes, this might be a problem but setting your rising bowl in a pan of warm water and putting the whole thing into an oven (the insulation will help to maintain the warmth) and adding warm water as needed should do the job. Please move your rising loaves out of the oven before you turn it on to preheat for baking!

Whole Wheat Bread

1¼ *pints water*	¼ *cup vegetable oil*
½ *cup honey*	1 *cup wheat germ*
¼ *teaspoon powdered ginger*	2 *teaspoons salt*
6 *pkgs. dry baking yeast (or 6 tablespoons)*	*about* 2½ *lbs. unsifted whole wheat flour*

Heat the water to 115°F. Have all other ingredients at room temperature.

Mix the honey and ginger with the warm water. Stir in the yeast. Cover and let stand in a warm place for about 10 minutes. The mixture should appear frothy; otherwise your yeast is dead and you'll have to begin again.

Add the oil, wheat germ and salt to the yeast mixture. Mix in half the flour and mix very well. Add more flour gradually, mixing with your hands to make a fairly stiff dough. Turn the dough out onto a well-floured board and knead until smooth and elastic, adding flour as needed.

Place the dough in a well-oiled bowl, and turn the dough to cover it with oil. Cover the dough and put it in a warm place to rise. The dough should be doubled in about 45 minutes.

Punch the dough down. Turn the punched side to the bottom of the bowl, cover, and let rise again for about 30 minutes. Turn the dough onto a floured board and let it rest for 10 minutes. Divide the dough into thirds and shape into three loaves. Place the loaves into well-oiled bread pans, cover and let rise in a warm place until nearly doubled.

Bake at 350°F. for about 40 minutes, or until the crust is brown and makes a hollow noise when you tap it.

Yield: 3 loaves.

Bran Bread

1 *tablespoon (1 package) dry yeast*	1 *teaspoon salt*
¾ *pint water at* 115°F.	1 *tablespoon vegetable oil*
2 *tablespoons honey*	1 *cup bran flakes*
	1 *lb. whole wheat flour*

Grease a 9″ bread pan.

Sprinkle the yeast over the warm water and stir in the honey. Cover and let stand in a warm place for about 5 minutes or until the yeast bubbles. (If the yeast doesn't bubble, start again.) All other ingredients should be at room temperature. Add the salt, oil and bran flakes. Slowly stir in the flour until the dough forms a mass. Turn the dough out onto a well-floured board and knead for about 5 minutes until smooth and elastic, adding flour as needed to keep the dough from sticking. Shape the dough into a fat cylinder and place it into the greased pan, seam side down. Cover with a clean cloth and let rise in a warm place until about doubled in bulk (about 45 minutes). Preheat oven to 350°F.

Gently brush the top of the loaf with oil. Bake the bread for 45–50 minutes or until done. Cool on a wire rack.
Makes one large loaf.

Wheat-Bran Bread
(A moist, dense bread with a delicious flavour.)

¾ *cup cracked wheat cereal*	3 *tablespoons honey*
1 *teaspoon salt*	⅓ *cup water at* 115°*F.*
12 *fl. oz. boiling water*	1 *tablespoon dry yeast*
4 *tablespoons oil*	½ *cup bran flakes*
2 *tablespoons molasses*	¾–1 *lb. whole wheat flour*

Mix together the cereal, salt, boiling water, oil, molasses and honey. Let stand until cooled to about 110°F.

Mix the ⅓ cup water with the yeast, cover and let stand for about 5 minutes or until the yeast bubbles.

Add the yeast mixture to the cooled cereal mixture. Stir in the bran flakes. Stir the wheat flour in gradually until the mixture is very thick but does not form a ball. Cover and let rise in a warm place 45 minutes.

Grease 2 loaf pans and sprinkle them with bread crumbs. Stir the dough, and divide it between the two pans. Cover and let rise in a warm place until about doubled (45 minutes – 1 hour). Preheat oven to 450°F. Put bread in oven, lower heat to 400°F., bake 50 minutes to 1 hour or until bread sounds hollow when tapped. Cool on a wire rack.

To make rolls, form dough into small balls, place in a greased pan with sides touching, let rise, and bake as for bread.

High Protein Whole Wheat Bread
3 loaves

Note: All ingredients should be at room temperature unless otherwise noted.

1¼ pints skimmed milk, scalded and cooled to 115°F.
½ cup molasses
pinch powdered ginger
2 oz. dried yeast
¼ cup vegetable oil
5 oz. soy flour
½ cup non-instant dry milk powder
½ cup lecithin powder
½ cup brewers' yeast powder
5 oz. gluten flour
2 oz. wheat germ
2 teaspoons salt
2–3 lbs. whole wheat flour, approximately

1. Stir the molasses and ginger into the milk. Add the yeast and stir just to mix. Cover the mixture with a cloth and let it rest in a warm place for about 10 minutes. At the end of 10 minutes, *the yeast should be bubbly.* If it is not, the yeast is dead and you must begin again.
2. Stir the vegetable oil into the yeast mixture.
3. In a large bowl, mix together the soy flour, milk powder, lecithin, brewers' yeast, gluten flour, wheat germ, salt and one lb. of the whole wheat flour. Mix well, then stir in the yeast mixture. Let it rest 10 minutes, as whole wheat flour absorbs moisture slowly and adding all the flour quickly might result in heavy bread.
4. Add flour to the mixture, one cup at a time, until the dough forms a fairly cohesive mass that can be lifted from the bowl.
5. Flour your kneading board well and place the mass of dough on the flour. Pat it into a roundish shape. Flour your hands. Press the heels of both hands into the dough mass at the centre, pushing away from your body. Lift your hands. With both hands, lift the edge of the dough furthest from you, and fold it toward you. It should fold nicely on the crease you made with the heels of your hands. You should now have a rough half circle of dough

with its diameter horizontal to you. Lift the mass of dough and give it a quarter turn so that the diameter is vertical to you. If the dough sticks to the board as you turn, sprinkle flour beneath it. Again, press the heels of both hands into the centre of the dough, pushing away. Fold the dough, give it a quarter turn. Flour if you need to. Press, push, fold, turn — that is all there is to kneading and you will soon develop a rhythm of your own. Add flour whenever the dough gets sticky, you may need to add quite a bit. As you knead, you will feel the dough becoming smooth and springy. It will reach a point where it no longer needs flour at every turn, it is fairly smooth and quite springy to the touch. At that point you may stop kneading. Roughly, it takes about 10 minutes of kneading to reach this point. Until your experience tells you the dough is done, you may let a clock be your guide.

6. Oil a large bowl. Pat the dough into a ball and place it in the bowl, turning it to cover all the surfaces lightly with oil. Cover with a cloth and set to rise in a warm place for about 45 minutes until it has doubled in bulk. To determine whether the dough has doubled, jab two fingers sharply into the centre of the dough, pressing down about $\frac{1}{2}$ inch. If the impressions remain, consider the dough doubled.

7. Push a fist into the centre of the dough ball — this is "punching down." Bring the edges of the dough toward the centre. Flour the kneading board. Turn the dough onto the floured board and let it rest 10 minutes.

8. While the dough rests, grease 3 breadpans.

9. Knead the dough 3 or 4 times to work out the largest air bubbles. With a sharp knife, divide the dough into roughly equal thirds. Push, pat and fold each third until it is somewhat loaf shaped. There will probably be a seam on one side of the loaf, so make sure that this side is at the bottom, and place your dough in the bread pan seam side down.

10. Cover the three loaves with a cloth and set them in your rising place for about 45 minutes or until doubled. You can *see* that the loaves have doubled, don't jab them

with your fingers or you'll have dented bread.
11. When the loaves have been rising for 35 minutes, preheat the oven to 350°F. (If your loaves were rising in the oven, you'll have to move them.)
12. Place the loaves in the oven, allowing space for air to circulate around them. Bake for *about* 45 minutes or until the top is brown and makes a hollow sound when you thump it.
13. Remove the bread from the pans immediately and cool on wire racks. Let the bread cool for at least 20 minutes before cutting it.

Carrot Bread

1¼ *pints carrot juice or veget-*
able water at 115°F.
¼ *cup molasses or black treacle*
3 *tablespoons yeast*
2 *teaspoons salt*
3 *tablespoons oil*

½ *cup wheat germ*
½ *cup gluten flour*
2 *lbs. whole wheat flour*
(approx.)
2 *cups grated carrots*

Add molasses to carrot juice, stir in yeast, cover and let stand 10 minutes or until the yeast is bubbly.

Add salt and oil to yeast mixture.

Mix wheat germ and gluten flour with 5 cups of whole wheat flour. Add flour mixture to yeast and beat well. Cover with cloth and set to rise for about 10 minutes.

Stir in carrots and add flour, a cup at a time until dough is workable. Knead on a floured board 10 minutes. Place dough in oiled bowl, turning to oil dough, cover and set to rise for about 45 minutes or until doubled.

Punch dough down. Turn out on a floured board and let rest for 10 minutes. Meanwhile, oil 3 bread pans.

Knead dough 3–4 times. Form 3 loaves. Place loaves seam side down in pans, cover and set to rise about 45 minutes.

During the last 10 minutes of rise, heat oven to 375°F. and bake about 30 minutes longer or until done. Remove from pans and cool on wire racks.

Herb Breadsticks
They go with everything!

1¼ cups skimmed milk, scalded
  and cooled to 115°F.
2 tablespoons honey
1½ tablespoons (¾ oz.) yeast
1 tablespoon vegetable oil
1½ teaspoons salt

2 teaspoons dried basil
1 teaspoon dried oregano
½ teaspoon pepper
dash garlic powder
1–1¼ lbs. whole wheat flour
  (approx.)

Add honey and yeast to milk. Stir to mix and let stand 10 minutes or until the yeast is bubbly.

Add oil, salt and herbs to yeast mixture. Stir to mix. Add 12 oz. of flour and let stand 10 minutes.

Add more flour, a cup at a time until the dough can be handled. Knead 10 minutes. Place the dough in an oiled bowl, turning to coat the dough with oil. Cover with a cloth and set to rise for 45 minutes or until doubled in bulk.

Punch the dough down. Let it rest on a floured board for 10 minutes. Knead 3–4 times.

Divide the dough in half. Roll each half into a rectangle about 12″ wide. Cut each rectangle into 12 sections. Roll each section between floured hands to make a baton about ⅓″ around and 12″ long.

Place the batons on an oiled baking sheet. Cover with a cloth and allow to rise until doubled in bulk, about 45 minutes.

During the last 10 minutes of rising, preheat the oven to 400°F.

Bake the breadsticks for about 15–20 minutes or until done.

Sandwich Rolls
A tasty hamburger bun

12 fl. ozs skimmed milk,
  scalded and cooled to
  115°F.

4 tablespoons honey
pinch powdered ginger
3 tablespoons yeast

⅓ *cup vegetable oil*   1–1½ *lbs. whole wheat flour*
1 *teaspoon salt*   *(approx.)*
2 *eggs, well beaten*

Mix together ½ cup of milk, 1 tablespoon of honey, ginger
and yeast. Cover and let rest 10 minutes or until yeast is
bubbly.

Add to yeast mixture the remaining milk and honey, oil,
salt, eggs and half of flour. Let stand 10 minutes.

Add flour, 1 cup at a time until the dough can be
kneaded.

On a floured board, knead dough 10 minutes or until
smooth and elastic. Place dough in oiled bowl, turn to oil
the dough, cover with cloth and set to rise for about 45
minutes or until doubled in bulk.

Punch down. Turn onto floured board and let rest 10
minutes. Knead 3–4 times. Cut dough into two pieces.
Roll each piece into a long cylinder. Cut about 2 inches
from end of one cylinder and pat into hamburger bun
shape. The piece you pat is roughly half the size of your
finished bun. Adjust size to your preference.

Place buns on greased baking sheet (or two). Cover
with cloth and let rise for about 45 minutes or until
doubled. During the last 10 minutes of rising, heat your
oven to 400°F.

Bake buns 15–20 minutes. Cool on wire racks.

Cheese Straws

½ *lb. whole wheat flour*   1 *cup grated sharp cheddar*
1 *oz. baking powder*   ¼ *pint milk (approx.)*
½ *teaspoon salt*   *sesame seeds (optional)*
3 *tablespoons oil*

Heat oven to 450°F.

Mix together the flour, baking powder and salt. Stir in
the oil. Stir in the cheese. Add milk gradually, stirring
with a fork until the dough forms a ball. Roll pieces of

dough between your hands to form sticks about ½″ wide and 6″ long. Roll sticks in sesame seeds if desired.

Place sticks on ungreased baking sheet and bake 10 to 12 minutes at 450°F. Cool on wire rack.

Makes about 24 straws.

Country Cornbread

½ *lb. whole wheat flour*	2 *tablespoons honey*
6 *oz. yellow cornmeal*	1 *egg, beaten*
1 *oz. baking powder*	½ *cup yogurt*
½ *teaspoon salt*	¼ *cup oil*

Heat oven to 425°F. Oil an 8″ × 8″ × 2″ tin.

Stir the dry ingredients together. Stir the liquid ingredients together and blend into the dry ingredients. Stir just to blend, do not overmix.

Bake at 425°F. 20–25 minutes.

Raisin-Nut Bread

¼ *lb. soy flour*	6 *oz. raisins*
6 *oz. whole wheat flour*	2 *eggs, lightly beaten*
2 *teaspoons baking powder*	6 *fl. oz. milk*
1 *teaspoon salt*	2 *tbs. honey*
½ *teaspoon cinnamon*	3 *tablespoons oil*
6 *oz. chopped nuts*	

Mix soy flour, wheat flour, baking powder, salt and cinnamon. Stir in nuts and raisins. Blend eggs with milk, honey and oil. Mix egg mixture into dry ingredients. Place dough in oiled pan and let rest 20 minutes. Heat oven to 325°F. and bake for 1 hour and 15 minutes or until done.

Walnut Tea Bread

2 *oz. whole wheat flour*	2 *eggs, beaten*
2 *oz. soy flour*	8 *fl. oz. buttermilk or yogurt*
1 *oz. baking powder*	2 *tablespoons vegetable oil*
½ *teaspoon bicarbonate of soda*	6 *oz. chopped walnuts*
½ *teaspoon allspice*	
1 *cup date sugar (or unrefined white)*	

Oil and flour 9″ loaf pan. Heat oven to 325°F. Sift together flours, baking powder, bicarbonate of soda, allspice. Stir in sugar. Mix together eggs, buttermilk and oil. Add to dry ingredients, stirring to mix. Mix in pecans. Pour mixture into loaf pan.

Bake at 325°F. for about 40 minutes or until a skewer comes out clean. Cool in pan for 10 minutes. Finish cooling on wire rack.

Rice Bread

¾ *lb. rice flour*	2 *egg yolks*
4 *oz. soy flour*	12 *fl. oz. soy milk, water or milk*
4 *tsp. baking powder*	
½ *teaspoon salt*	2 *tbs. honey*
2 *egg whites*	4 *tablespoons vegetable oil*

Oil a loaf pan. Heat oven to 325°F.

Mix dry ingredients thoroughly. Beat egg whites until stiff but not dry. In a separate bowl, beat the yolks until creamy. Add the milk, honey and oil, and mix well. Add the yolk mixture to the dry ingredients stirring, until smooth. Fold in the egg whites gently. Place mixture in prepared pan, and bake at 325°F. for about 1½ hours or until brown. Cool on a wire rack.

Banana-Bran Tea Bread

⅔ teacup mashed ripe bananas   2½ teaspoons bicarbonate of
3 tbs. honey   soda
2 eggs   6 oz. whole wheat flour
½ teaspoon cinnamon   2½ oz. chopped walnuts
1 oz. bran

Heat oven to 350°F. Grease a loaf pan.

Mix ingredients in order. Place the mixture into the prepared pan and let stand at room temperature for 20 minutes. Bake 45 minutes to 1 hour or until a skewer comes out clean. Cool on a wire rack.

Sesame Wafers
(Version One)

6 oz. whole wheat flour   1 cup toasted sesame seeds
⅓ cup soy flour   ⅓ to ½ cup iced water
4 tablespoons sesame tahini

Heat oven to 300°F.

Mix flours together. Add tahini and mix with your hands until mixture resembles fine meal. Mix in sesame seeds. Add iced water a little at a time until dough will form a ball.

Roll dough on a floured board to ⅛″ thick. Cut into rounds, squares or diamonds. Scraps may be re-rolled.

Bake wafers on an ungreased baking sheet for 15–20 minutes or until crisp (they won't brown very much). Cool on a wire rack.

Makes about 8 dozen 1½ inch rounds or 6 dozen 2 inch rounds.
Store in an airtight jar or tin.

Sesame Wafers
(Version Two)

After you have mixed the tahini into the flours, add 1 teaspoon salt and ½ teaspoon powdered garlic. Continue as above.

Try varying these recipes with your favourite herbs and spices.

Wheatless Crackers

3 oz. soy flour
1 teaspoon celery salt
1 egg, beaten
1 tablespoon milk

½ cup grated cheese (mature
   Cheddar)
¼ cup sesame seeds

Oil a baking sheet. Pre-heat oven to 350°F.

Mix soy flour and salt. Stir in egg and milk. Stir in cheese, mixing well. Roll out to ¼″ thickness on a floured board. Sprinkle with sesame seeds and roll lightly to press the seeds in. Cut into 1½″ squares. Place on oiled sheet and bake at 350°F. for about 20 minutes or until lightly browned.

Makes about 2 dozen.

Pumpkinseed Wafers

1½ teacups pumpkinseeds
2 tablespoons oil
1 teaspoon salt

2 oz. soy flour
6 oz. whole wheat flour
⅓ to ½ cup iced water

Heat oven to 300°F.

Grind or pulverize in a blender ½ cup of pumpkinseeds. Mix oil and salt with ground seeds. Mix in flours with a fork until mixture resembles fine meal. Add water, a little at a time, mixing until dough forms a ball.

Roll dough on floured board to thickness of about ⅛

inch. Cut into squares, rounds or diamonds.

Bake on ungreased baking sheet for 20 minutes. (They do not brown very much). Cool on a wire rack.

Makes about 6 dozen 2-inch squares.

Snacking Crackers

1 *lb. rolled oats*
6 *oz. soy flour*
½ *teaspoon seasoned salt*

½ *teaspoon powdered kelp*
1 *cup milk*
½ *cup oil*

GARNISH
½ *teaspoon coarse salt*
½ *cup sesame seeds*

Toast the coarse salt and sesame seeds together in a heavy frying pan until the seeds are beginning to brown slightly. Remove the mixture immediately to a plate and set aside.

Heat oven to 400°F. Oil two baking sheets.

Mix together the oats, soy flour, seasoned salt and kelp. Beat the oil and milk together and add to the oat mixture gradually while stirring. Knead the mixture slightly and divide into two portions. Place a portion on each of the prepared baking sheets. Roll thin with a small glass. Brush the surface of the dough lightly with water and sprinkle on the sesame salt mixture. Pat down gently. With a sharp knife, divide the dough into rectangles, triangles or diamonds.

Place baking sheets in oven and reduce heat immediately to 325°F. Bake about 25 minutes or until very slightly browned. Turn off the oven, and let the crackers rest in the oven with the door open for about 5 minutes more. Remove from the oven, loosen the crackers with a spatula and allow them to cool on the baking sheets.

Sour Cream Pastry
for two crusts

3 *tablespoons sour cream*	$\frac{1}{2}$ *teaspoon salt*
2 *eggs*	$\frac{1}{2}$ *cup oil*
14 *oz. flour*	

Put the sour cream in a small bowl. Add the eggs and beat to mix.

Add the salt to the flour and mix, stir in the oil until the mixture resembles coarse bread crumbs. Stir in the sour cream-egg mixture. Mix to make a ball of dough. Wrap the ball in waxed paper and refrigerate for at least half-an-hour.

Pie Pastry
for one crust

5–6 *oz. whole wheat flour*	1–3 *tablespoons cold milk or*
$\frac{1}{4}$ *cup oil*	*water*
1 *egg*	

Mix oil and egg together with 1 tablespoon of milk or water. Stir mixture into flour. Add more liquid if needed. The dough should form a ball.

Place ball of dough in pie dish, and pat into place.

Super Mix
For pancakes, waffles, muffins or scones

12 *oz. whole wheat flour*	2 *oz. cornmeal*
4 *oz. soy flour*	2 *oz. brown rice flour*
4 *oz. buckwheat flour*	$\frac{1}{2}$ *cup brewers' yeast*
2 *oz. wheat germ*	$\frac{1}{2}$ *cup powdered lecithin*
4 *oz. roasted peanut flour* (optional)	

Mix all of the above ingredients together. Keep in the

refrigerator or freezer until used. We made the peanut flour optional because it might be hard to find, but it is definitely worth hunting for.

Super Pancakes

4 oz. super mix	2 tablespoons honey
pinch salt	2 eggs
1½ teaspoons baking powder	¾ cup skimmed milk (about)
2 tablespoons oil	

Combine ingredients in order and cook pancakes on a hot oiled griddle.
Serves 4.

Super Waffles
Same as super pancakes, but increase the milk to 1 cup (about), and cook on a waffle iron.

Bran Griddle Scones

1 egg	1 oz. whole wheat flour
½ cup plain yogurt	¼ teaspoon baking powder
1 oz. bran	

Beat the egg and yogurt together.
Add the bran and flour and mix well.
Heat a griddle over moderate heat and brush lightly with oil. Add the baking powder to the batter and mix well. Cook until evenly golden on both sides.
Makes 6 medium griddle scones.

American Breakfast Muffins

7 oz. whole wheat flour	¼ pint milk
½ teaspoon kelp	2 eggs, lightly beaten
2 oz. soy flour	2 tablespoons safflower oil
½ cup non-instant powdered milk	4 tablespoons molasses
	3 oz. raisins
2 tsp. baking powder	¼ cup sunflower seeds

Oil 16 patty pans. Heat oven to 375°F.

Mix together the flour, salt, soy flour, powdered milk and baking powder. Stir in the milk, eggs, oil and molasses until smooth. Mix in the raisins and sunflower seeds. Fill each patty pan about ⅔ full. Bake about 20 minutes at 375°F. Turn out the muffins and serve hot or cool on a wire rack.

Makes about 16 muffins.

Easy Scones

3 oz. whole wheat flour	1 teaspoon baking powder
2 oz. soy flour	2 tablespoons oil
1 oz. wheat germ	⅓ cup plain yogurt (about)
pinch salt	

Heat oven to 450°F. Oil a baking tray.

Mix the dry ingredients together thoroughly. Stir in the oil, then add the yogurt, a little at a time to make a soft dough for drop scones or a stiff dough for rolled scones.

Roll stiff dough out on a floured board and cut into rounds. Soft dough may be dropped by rounded teaspoonful onto the prepared baking tray.

Bake the scones for 8 to 10 minutes or until the tops are just beginning to brown. Serve immediately.

Makes about 10 small scones. Double the recipe, if desired.

American Whole Wheat Muffins

$\frac{1}{4}$ *pint milk*
1 *egg*
2 *tbs. honey*
1 *oz. wheat germ*
2 *oz. soy flour*
4 *oz. wheat flour*

$\frac{3}{4}$ *teaspoon salt*
3 *teaspoons baking powder*
2 *tablespoons oil*
$\frac{1}{2}$ *cup cooked whole wheat berries, bulghur or kasha (optional)*

Heat oven to 400°F. Oil 16 patty pans.

Beat together the milk, egg and honey. Add the wheat germ and let stand for about 3 minutes. Stir in the oil. Sift together the soy flour, whole wheat flour, salt and baking powder. Stir into the milk mixture. Stir in the wheat berries.

Fill prepared patty pans half full. Bake for 20–25 minutes.

Sauce-ery – Magic in the Kitchen

In the great restaurants of the world, there are chefs who do nothing except make sauces. That is not too surprising when you consider that the secret ingredient in many fine dishes is an excellent and subtle sauce. Sometimes it may be the addition of a little Espagnole sauce to a gravy or soup for an ineffable touch of richness. At other times, one might simply use a white or Béchamel sauce to bring together some too-good-to-discard leftovers. A good sauce should not only stand on its own, but should make a definite contribution to any dish to which it is added.

As you perfect your own repertoire of sauces, you will find that almost every sauce lends itself to the personal variation. Your favourite herb or spice can enhance your sauce in a way that is entirely your own. Learning to use sauces can not only expand your culinary horizons, but allow you to make a personal statement at the same time.

Sauces as simple as White Sauce, Béchamel and Vinaigrette are so quick and easy to make, that you need not trouble to have them on hand, although White and Béchamel can be frozen (thaw before heating), and Vinaigrette keeps very well in the refrigerator. The more complicated sauces do, however, take considerably more time. If you have freezer space, you can keep a supply of both brown and white stock on hand to use as needed. Stock is not a sauce, but it *is* the basic ingredient in many of the finest sauces. It is not a good idea to use tinned broth or bouillon in place of homemade stock, as the flavour is vastly different, and can spoil a potentially good sauce.

Espagnole is, admittedly, a complex and time-consuming sauce, but it is worth every minute. It also freezes very well. It is the base of nearly every classic brown sauce and is invaluable for enhancing soups, stews and gravies.

White Sauce with Cheese (Mornay), or Velouté Sauce with Mustard can make a dull vegetable sparkle. Leftover vegetables that have not been overcooked in the first place can be marinated in vinaigrette. Another variation is to make a Velouté Sauce using vegetable cooking water in place of stock, then adding the cooked diced vegetable, any diced, cooked meat and sieved hard-boiled egg for colour and texture.

Speaking of colour, we've taken a few liberties with the classic recipes, such as using whole wheat flour instead of refined flour. That means that your "white" sauces will be a sort of creamy colour, anyway. Besides, the taste of a sauce made with whole wheat flour is much more satisfying than one made with tasteless white flour. We have also substituted oil for butter wherever possible. A little cream can enrich a sauce, but in most cases, non-fat milk works very well.

When it comes to using sauces, be inventive. A White or Béchamel sauce added to puréed vegetables and a little vegetable cooking water can produce a very respectable cream soup. Vinaigrette sauce is really nothing more than seasoned oil and vinegar dressing, infinitely variable. Try a little sauce-ery in *your* kitchen.

Brown Stock

3 *lbs. meaty beef bones, prefer-ably shinbones*	1 *large sprig parsley*
	generous pinch thyme
2 *onions, in chunks*	5 *peppercorns*
2 *carrots, in chunks*	1 *teaspoon salt*
1 *leafy stalk celery, in chunks*	1 *teaspoon soy sauce*
1 *bay leaf*	7 *pints water*

Place the bones in a large, heavy pot. (Do not use enamelware.) Allow the bones to brown over very low heat for 15–20 minutes, turning occasionally. Add oil only if absolutely necessary. Add the vegetables and brown them lightly. Add all remaining ingredients. Bring slowly to the boil, skimming as necessary. Partly cover the pan and simmer 4–5 hours. Strain.

White Stock

White stock is prepared similarly to Brown Stock with these important differences: only veal bones are used, and soy sauce is omitted. Place the veal bones in a large pot and add everything *except* the vegetables. Bring slowly to a boil, skim thoroughly, *then* add the vegetables. Partly cover and simmer 4–5 hours as for brown stock. Strain.

Basic White Sauce

1 *oz. butter*	8 *fl. oz. skimmed milk*
1 *tablespoon whole wheat flour*	*salt and white pepper to taste*

Melt the butter in a small pan. Off the heat, stir in the flour. Blend in half of the milk. Over low heat, blend in the remaining milk and cook, stirring, until it reaches the boil. Simmer 1–2 minutes, then season to taste with salt and pepper.

Cheese Sauce

2 *oz. grated cheese*	1 *cup white sauce, or Béchamel*
½ *teaspoon prepared mustard*	*sauce*
(preferably Dijon-style)	

Stir grated cheese into freshly-made, hot white sauce. When well mixed, stir in the mustard. If sauce seems too thick, stir in a little hot milk.

Béchamel Sauce

8 *fl. oz. skimmed milk*   *pinch powdered mace*
1 *slice onion about ¼ inch thick*   1 *oz. butter*
1 *bay leaf*   ½ *oz. whole wheat flour*
4 *peppercorns*   *salt and white pepper to taste*

Heat the milk to just below the boiling point. Add the onion, bay leaf, peppercorns and mace. Heat milk, but do not boil. Strain milk and set aside. Melt the butter in a small pan and stir in the flour. Stir in half of the milk. Over low heat, whisk in the remaining milk. Bring to a boil, stirring, and allow to simmer 2 minutes while stirring.

Velouté Sauce

1 *oz. butter*   2 *fl. oz. milk or single cream*
½ *oz. whole wheat flour*   *salt and white pepper to taste*
8 *fl. oz. white stock*

Heat the butter and stir in the flour. Add half of the stock and whisk to mix well. Whisk in the remaining stock and stir at a simmer for two minutes. Stir in the milk or cream and season to taste.

Variations: Add 1 tablespoon dried capers and 1 tablespoon chopped parsley — serve with fish. Add 1 teaspoon Dijon-style mustard.

Sauce Espagnole

6 *tablespoons vegetable oil*   2 *mushrooms, finely chopped*
1 *onion, finely diced*   2 *pints brown stock*
1 *carrot, finely diced*   1 *bay leaf*
1 *stalk celery, finely diced*   1 *sprig parsley*
2 *tablespoons whole wheat*   *pinch thyme*
  flour   *salt and pepper to taste*
1 *teaspoon tomato paste*

Heat the oil over low heat and sauté the onion, carrot and celery until the vegetables are soft. Stir in the flour while browning lightly. Stir in the tomato paste, mushrooms and four cups of stock. Add the herbs. Bring to a boil and skim. Cover partly and simmer over low heat for about 30 minutes. Add ½ cup stock, bring to boil, skim, simmer 5 minutes, add remaining stock, return to boil, skim again and simmer 5 minutes more. Strain through a cheesecloth-lined sieve, pressing vegetables gently to extract all the juices. Place strained sauce in a clean pan. Partly cover and simmer over very low heat until sauce is reduced to about ¾ pint. Sauce may be frozen.

Vinaigrette Sauce

¼ *cup wine, tarragon or cider vinegar*
¾ *cup light vegetable oil*
½ *teaspoon Dijon-style mustard*

1 *teaspoon fresh or* ½ *teaspoon dried herbs (thyme, basil, marjoram, parsley, chervil, etc.)*

Put everything together in a jar and shake until thoroughly mixed. Add a little salt and pepper if needed.

Makes 1 cup. Vinaigrette keeps well in the refrigerator.

Variations: Add a clove of garlic squished through a press. Replace all or part of the vinegar with lemon juice.

Fresh Tomato Sauce

2 *tablespoons oil*
1 *medium onion, finely chopped*
2 *cloves garlic, minced*

1 *lb. tomatoes (preferably Italian) peeled, seeded, and chopped*
½ *teaspoon basil*
2 *tablespoons chopped parsley*

Heat the oil in a large frying pan. Add the onion and garlic and sauté until onion is translucent. Add the remaining

ingredients. Simmer for 10 minutes or until thick, stirring
occasionally.
  Makes about ½ pint.

Sesame Seasoning Paste

½ cup toasted sesame seeds   *2 tablespoons finely chopped*
2 tablespoons soy sauce   *parsley*
1 tablespoon brewers' yeast   *2 tablespoons water*
1 spring onion, minced

Coarsely purée all ingredients in a blender. Use to season
salad dressings, soups, sandwich spreads, or meat loaves
and hamburgers. Thin with yogurt to make a dip.

Mineral Mayonnaise

1 soft egg* (see page   ) do not   *1 tablespoon brewers' yeast*
  shell the egg!   *½ teaspoon vegetable salt*
2 tablespoons vinegar**   *4 fl. oz. vegetable oil*
1 clove garlic, crushed   *2 fl. oz. olive oil*

* If you don't HAVE a soft egg, use any fresh egg, but remove and
discard the shell.
** Preferably, use "soft egg" vinegar, but any cider or rice vinegar
will do.

Place the egg, vinegar, garlic, yeast and salt in a blender.
Mix the oils. Add ¼ cup oil to the stuff in the blender, and
blend until well mixed. With the blender on medium
speed, add the remaining oil slowly, until it is all
absorbed, and you have a thick mayonnaise. Chill.
NOTE: Vary by adding fresh parsley or any fresh herb to the egg mixture.

Sorrel Sauce

2 oz. shredded, stemmed sorrel   *1 small container yogurt*
½ oz. butter

Heat butter and sorrel together and cook over very low heat until very soft. Stir in the yogurt.

Pesto

1 *oz. grated pecorino or Parmesan cheese*	2 *cups packed fresh basil leaves*
4 *cloves minced garlic*	$\frac{1}{4}$ *cup chopped parsley*
$\frac{1}{4}$ *cup pine nuts*	$\frac{1}{2}$ *cup olive oil or half olive, half safflower*

Process the cheese, garlic, nuts, basil and parsley in a blender until the mixture resembles a coarse paste. Drizzle in the oil to mix well. Pesto will keep indefinitely if refrigerated in a glass jar and protected from air with a layer of olive oil.

Pesto may be made in a blender, but the original way is to make it by hand with a mortar and pestle, which is time consuming, but pleasant — and rewarding.

Mayonnaise 1
(By hand)

2 *egg yolks*	2 *fl. oz. olive oil*
$\frac{1}{2}$ *teaspoon powdered mustard*	4 *fl. oz. safflower oil*
2 *teaspoons vinegar*	1 *tablespoon lemon juice*

Have all ingredients at room temperature.

In a large bowl, beat eggs until thick and lemon-coloured. Beat in mustard and $\frac{1}{2}$ teaspoon of the vinegar. Mix the oils together. Beat in $\frac{1}{2}$ of the oil mixture, adding just a little at a time. The mixture should thicken.

Mix the remaining vinegar with the lemon juice. Drop by drop, add the vinegar mixture alternately with the oil mixture, beating constantly. The result should be thick and smooth.

If it curdles, beat another egg yolk and beat in the curdled mayonnaise, drop by drop.

Mayonnaise 11
(Using blender)

1 *whole egg*
2 *tablespoons lemon juice*
¼ *teaspoon paprika*
1 *tablespoon chopped chives*

4 *fl. oz. olive oil*
2 *fl. oz. sunflower oil*
2 *fl. oz. safflower oil*

Put egg, lemon juice, paprika and chives in blender and blend for a few seconds just to mix.

Mix the oils together. Add ⅓ of the oil mixture to the blender and blend. The mixture should be thick and creamy. With the blender on low speed, trickle in as much of the remaining oil as the mixture will incorporate. You may not need all of the oil.

Variation: Add ½ or 1 teaspoon of a favourite herb, minced, or a squish of garlic to the egg mixture.

NOTE: Mayonnaise contains raw egg yolk and should be refrigerated as soon as it is made. It should be used within two or three days.

Beef Mushroom Sauce for Pasta

2 *tablespoons oil*
1 *onion, minced*
1 *lb. minced beef*
½ *lb. fresh mushrooms, chopped*
2 *cloves garlic, crushed*

1 *cup red wine*
1 *teaspoon basil*
1 *teaspoon marjoram*
salt and pepper to taste
2 *tablespoons minced parsley*

Heat the oil and sauté the onion until translucent. Add the minced beef and stir until the meat is browned and separated. Add the mushrooms, garlic, wine, basil and marjoram. Simmer, stirring occasionally until the mixture is thick — about 30 minutes. Season to taste. Serve over cooked pasta and top with the parsley.

Makes enough sauce for 4 portions.

Mornay Sauce

1 *oz. butter*
½ *oz. whole wheat flour*
8 *fl. oz. hot milk*
salt & pepper to taste
dash of nutmeg (optional)

½ *cup grated cheddar cheese*
½ *teaspoon Worcestershire sauce*
½ *teaspoon prepared mustard (optional)*

Melt butter over medium heat, add the flour and mix well. Stir in the milk, salt and pepper. Simmer, stirring for 4 or 5 minutes or until mixture thickens. Off heat, stir in cheese, Worcestershire sauce and mustard.

Serve over cooked vegetables, poached eggs, cooked seafood, etc.

Mushroom Sauce

6 *oz. sliced mushrooms*
2 *oz butter*
2 *spring onions, chopped*
1 *oz. whole wheat flour*

8 *fl. oz. milk*
freshly ground nutmeg, salt and pepper to taste

Melt the butter and sauté the mushrooms and spring onions until limp. Add the whole wheat flour. Cook and stir for a minute more. Gradually add the milk while stirring. Cook, stirring until sauce thickens. Season to taste with nutmeg, salt and pepper.

Serves 6.

Prawn Sauce for Pasta

1 *oz. butter*
2 *tablespoons oil*
1½ *lbs. raw prawns, shelled and deveined*
salt and pepper
2 *tablespoons minced shallots*

2 *tbs. tomato purée*
½ *cup plain yogurt*
½ *teaspoon dried basil*
1 *egg yolk, lightly beaten*
1 *tablespoon plain yogurt*
2 *tablespoons chopped parsley*

Heat butter and oil, add prawns and sauté until brightly coloured. Sprinkle with salt and pepper to taste and add the shallots. Stir well. Add tomato purée, ½ cup yogurt and basil. Heat to simmer. Mix egg yolk with 1 tablespoon plain yogurt and add to the sauce, stirring rapidly. Do not allow sauce to boil. Remove from heat and pour sauce over freshly cooked pasta. Sprinkle with parsley.

Serves 4.

Soy Butter
An interesting and delicious spread

¼ *cup soy oil*
¾ *cup soy flour*

Mix together. Season to taste with vegetable salts, herbs or spices. Chopped nuts or seeds may be added.

Poly-Butter

¼ *lb. butter*
2 *fl. oz. oil*

Let butter come to room temperature, then mix in the oil. Put in a pretty crock and refrigerate. Use like ordinary butter. Add a bit of seasoned salt or minced fresh herbs for flavour.

Walnut Sauce for Pasta

6 *oz. shelled walnuts*
1 *clove garlic*
2 *tablespoons safflower oil*
2 *tablespoons water*
1 *tablespoon olive oil*
2 *tablespoons lemon juice*
salt to taste

Put walnuts, garlic and safflower oil in blender and blend

to a paste. (You may use a mortar and pestle, if you prefer.) Put paste in small saucepan and heat gently, while stirring in remaining ingredients. If sauce is too thick, you may add more water.

Serve hot over cooked whole wheat or spinach pasta. *Serves 4.*

Ragtag Relish

2 tomatoes, peeled, seeded and chopped
1 large onion, finely chopped
1 green pepper, seeded and finely chopped
1 carrot, peeled and finely chopped

1 small cucumber, peeled, seeded and finely chopped
1 teaspoon salt
3 tbs. honey
2 teaspoons cornflour
½ cup cider vinegar
½ teaspoon pepper

Place vegetables in a pot and add the salt. Cover with cold water and bring to a boil. Remove from heat and drain vegetables, reserving the liquid for soup. Mix together the honey, cornflour, vinegar and pepper. Bring to a boil. Add the vegetables and simmer 3 to 5 minutes or until the vegetables are tender. Let cool. Chill.

All-Soy "White" Sauce
The soy flour actually makes it an appetizing golden colour

2 tablespoons oil
2 oz. soy flour

8 fl. oz. stock or water
½ teaspoon lecithin

In a 3-pint saucepan, heat the oil and add the soy flour, stir with a wire whisk and add the stock while stirring over medium heat. Bring to a boil (it will foam) reduce the heat and simmer for about five minutes. Add the liquid lecithin, and stir with a whisk until the sauce is thick. Add seasoning to taste. Vegetable salt is very good. Sautéed minced onion adds a nice texture, as do sautéed mushrooms.

Makes about 1 cup. Use as a sauce or gravy.

Tomato Sauce

2 *onions, minced*
1 *carrot, minced*
1 *stalk celery, minced*
1 *clove garlic, minced*
2 *tablespoons oil*

2 *pints home-bottled tomatoes*
1 *teaspoon basil*
pinch fennel
salt and pepper to taste

Sauté the onion, carrot, celery and garlic in the oil for 5–10 minutes or until soft. Add the tomatoes, basil and fennel and simmer 20 minutes. Season to taste.

Tomato Sauce with Meat

1 *lb. minced beef*
1 *tablespoon vegetable oil*
1 *oz. whole wheat flour*
4 *onions, chopped finely*
2 *carrots, chopped finely*
2 *cloves garlic, minced*
3 *pints tinned tomatoes*

$\frac{1}{2}$ *cup red wine or water*
1 *bay leaf*
$\frac{1}{4}$ *teaspoon powdered fennel*
$\frac{1}{2}$ *teaspoon basil*
$\frac{1}{2}$ *cup soy powder*
$\frac{1}{2}$ *cup wheat germ*
salt and pepper to taste

Heat the oil in a heavy pot and add the meat, stirring to brown. Add the flour and stir to brown lightly, then add the onions, carrots and garlic, mixing well. Add the tomatoes and their liquid, breaking the tomatoes into small pieces with the spoon as you stir. Add the wine or water, bay leaf, fennel and basil. Cover and simmer for an hour.

Add the soy powder and wheat germ. Taste for seasoning.

Bottling Tomatoes

The skins of tomatoes, when cooked, resemble something between leather and rubber. They are palatable in dishes in which the tomato is cooked more or less intact and for not too long a time. Otherwise, the skins are simple to remove if the tomatoes are ripe.

To Peel Tomatoes — Dip *ripe* tomatoes in boiling water for ten seconds. Dip in cold water. Remove the stem end. The skins will peel off easily. If the tomatoes are less than fully ripe or have green spots, they will not peel.

To Bottle Tomatoes — It takes about three pounds of tomatoes for two pints. You will need a large heavy pot with a rack, deep enough to cover the jars you will be using with about three inches of boiling water. You will also need sufficient clean bottling jars filled with very hot water to heat them and clean, new lids for the jars.

Heat the water in your large pot to a simmering boil. Pack tomatoes into the hot, empty jars to within one-half inch of the top, pressing gently to fill the spaces. The tomatoes may be peeled, or the peelings may be removed when the jars are opened for use. Add one-half teaspoon of salt for a pint, one teaspoon for a quart. Wipe jar tops to remove any spills. Adjust the lids. Place the jars in the pot. If the water does not cover the bars by about three inches, add boiling water. From the time that the water resumes boiling, pint jars should be kept at simmer (212°F.) for 35 minutes, quart jars for 45 minutes. Remove jars from pot to a dry surface (we use a terry towel to be sure.) Complete seals unless your jars are the self-closing type.

Tomato Juice, Purée, Sauce and Ketchup for Bottling

It takes about five pounds of tomatoes for two pints of juice *and* two pints of purée. The tomatoes need not be as perfect as those used for bottling.

Wash the tomatoes and place them in a very large pan. Slice the tomatoes in the pan and mash them somewhat. Set the pan over very high heat. Add about one teaspoon of salt for every four pounds of tomatoes. Cover the pan. Bring to a boil, cook five or ten minutes or until tender. Cooking time will depend on the ripeness of the tomatoes.

Place a sieve over a deep bowl. Pour the contents of the pan onto the sieve. Collect the juice that pours off and set it aside. Mash the pulp through the sieve to make a thick purée. We find the juice rather thin and like to add a quarter cup of purée to each two pints of juice. The juice may be bottled in sterile jars while still hot. Process as for bottled tomatoes, 10 minutes for either pint or quart. Juice may also be used to fill any spaces in the jars when bottling tomatoes.

The purée may be bottled as it is. Process 35 minutes for a pint, 45 minutes for two pints.

Purée may be flavoured for sauce. We prefer to flavour the purée after opening, with one exception. When basil and tomatoes are ripe at the same time, we chop fresh basil leaves — about one teaspoon for each pint — and crush one clove of garlic for each pint, too, to make an Italian style sauce. Bottle as for purée.

Purée may also be made into ketchup.

Rather than cook the purée, we cook the ketchup spices and add them to the purée. It may be unorthodox, but it is also the most delicious and least-cooked ketchup we know.

Ketchup Spices
(For two pints)

1 *medium onion, minced*	1 *cinnamon stick (about 3″)*
¼ *cup cider vinegar*	8 *whole allspice*
½ *teaspoon celery seed*	2 *tablespoons honey*

Mix the spices together, bring to a boil and simmer five minutes. Strain, add to purée. Add another tablespoonful of honey and bring the purée to a boil. If you think it should be thicker, you may simmer it, stirring until it is as thick as you wish. But the *less* you cook it, the *better* it will be. If you like your ketchup a little hot, you may add a pinch of cayenne to the spice mixture.

Bottle the ketchup as for purée.

Green Tomatoes

Delicious pickles and relishes may be made from green tomatoes. It is a traditional way of using up the last green fruits before the first frost. Rather than trust that there will be enough in the autumn, we make pickles all summer and usually have plenty to give our friends. Pickles are not only good to eat, they have Vitamin C and minerals as well.

Some pickle-making processes require soaking the ingredients in salt water for several hours and discarding the water. Obviously you are also discarding some vitamins and minerals. The soaking is to ensure crispness. Since it is not used in *all* of our pickle-making, we choose to sacrifice nutrition in favour of crispness in a few recipes. Pickles are, after all, a side dish. Sugar and salt are both preservatives for bottling. We have substituted honey successfully in bottling some fruits, but find that sugar is more compatible with pickles.

NOTE: *Never* use anything but pure salt, free of all additives, in pickle-making. Additives will make your pickles cloudy.

Green Tomato Chutney

10–12 *medium green toma-*
toes, cut in one-inch chunks
1 *hot red pepper, seeded and*
chopped small
1 *lemon, seeds removed, chop-*
ped small
½ *cup fresh ginger root, chopped*
small

1½ *cups raisins*
2 *cloves garlic, peeled and*
chopped
2¼ *cups light brown sugar*
2 *cups cider vinegar*
1½ *teaspoon salt*
pinch cayenne, if desired

Mix all ingredients and simmer 15 minutes or until the
tomatoes are tender. Pack into hot, sterilized jars. Seal.
Process in boiling water for five minutes.

Yield: About 3 pints.

Piccalilli
Goes With Everything!

22 *medium green tomatoes*
8–10 *onions*
12 *sweet peppers, as ripe and*
red as possible
1¼ *pints cider vinegar*
1¼ *lbs. sugar*

¼ *teaspoon salt*
1½ *teaspoon allspice*
1½ *teaspoon cinnamon*
3½ *teaspoons celery seeds*
½ *cup mustard seeds*

Remove the stem end from the tomatoes and cut them into
quarters. Coarsely chop the tomatoes, onions and peppers
together using a food processor.

Mix the spices, sugar and salt with the vinegar and
bring to a boil. Add the chopped vegetables and simmer
15 minutes.

Pack into hot, sterilized jars. Seal. Process in boiling
water (212°F.) for five minutes.

Yield: About five pints.

Green Tomato Pickles

20 *medium green tomatoes*
2 *tablespoons salt*
¾ *pint cider vinegar*
5 *oz. sugar*
3 *tablespoons mustard seeds*
½ *teaspoon celery seed*

½ *teaspoon tumeric*
3 *large onions, sliced thin*
2 *sweet peppers, preferably red, in thin strips*
1 *tablespoon minced hot red pepper (may be omitted)*

Remove the stem end from the tomatoes and slice them about ¼ inch thick. Toss with the salt and let stand in a glass or enamel container for 12 hours. Drain.

Heat the vinegar, sugar and spices to a boil. Add the onions and simmer three minutes. Add the drained tomatoes and peppers and simmer five minutes more, stirring gently once or twice. Pack the mixture into hot, sterilized jars. Seal. Process in boiling water for five minutes.

Yield: About three pints.

Fresh Juices
& Beverages

When fresh fruits and vegetables are at their abundant best there are numerous varieties from which to choose, and an opportunity for even the most city-bound among us to find fresh, unsprayed produce as local wares come to market. *Unsprayed* is essential, for while you might not sit down and eat 10 carrots at a time, it's rather easy to *drink* 10 carrots. If you cannot find unsprayed produce, be sure to wash very carefully and remove skins and rinds whenever you can although, often, vitamins and minerals are concentrated in the skin.

As you begin your juice adventure, your first discovery will be that the taste is not what you expected. Beetroot juice is *sweet*. Lettuce juice is slightly *bitter*. Celery juice is *salty*. Fresh tomato juice has very little in common with the tinned variety. For beginners, I suggest juicing each component separately, then mixing them to taste. I *don't* dis-assemble and clean the juicer between each vegetable though — not until I've finished the juice-combination I'm working on.

Herbs can add a sparkling taste to juices, but please remember that they are potent and should be used in *small* amounts, as accents.

Some juices have more pulp than others. As a general rule, the softer the fruit or vegetable, the pulpier the juice. Pulp is no detriment, but the juice will have a tendency to separate. Just stir it up with a carrot, celery stick or pineapple spear.

You can expand the horizons of juices, too, by thinking of them as not just juices, but frozen desserts, cold soups or iced lollies.

Juices bring you enzymes in a glass, with a lot of

vitamins and minerals. Juices do not provide fibre or essential fatty acids, however, so a diet that relies heavily on juices should include some fibre foods and polyunsaturated fats as well as Vitamins D, E and B-Complex. While vegetables and fruits can be good sources of trace minerals, the amount of available mineral will depend on the soil where they're grown. I like to sprinkle some juices with a little kelp for extra mineral-power.

Once you begin concocting your own fresh juice combinations, you won't want to stop. One combination leads to another, and another, and another . . .

Grape Cocktail

$\frac{1}{2}$ *cup grape juice*
$\frac{1}{2}$ *teaspoon lemon juice*

We juiced whole, dark-skinned grapes, not seeded. It would be difficult to specify the exact amount of grapes needed as some are juicier than others.

Tall Green Treat

2 *stalks celery, with leaves*
1 *small courgette*
1 *green pepper, seeded*

2 *tablespoons fresh, chopped parsley*

Juice everything together. Add fresh lemon juice to taste, if desired.

Tomato Treat

5 *tomatoes*
2 *stalks celery, with leaves*

1 *tablespoon chopped fresh parsley*
1 *tablespoon fresh lemon juice*

Juice the tomatoes, celery and parsley together. Stir in the lemon juice.

Fruit Cooler

pulp from ½ ripe melon	*½ small apple, cored*
1 *carrot*	*½ cup grapefruit juice*
4 *or* 5 *strawberries*	*¼ teaspoon fresh lemon juice*

Juice together the melon pulp, carrot, berries and apple. Mix with the grapefruit and lemon juices.

Vegetable Cooler

2 *stalks celery, with leaves*	1 *tablespoon chopped fresh parsley*
2 *carrots*	
3 *medium apples, cored*	1 *tablespoon fresh lemon juice*

Juice together the celery, carrots, apples and parsley. Stir in the lemon juice.

Berry Delight

½ cup strawberries	1 *small carrot*
2 *small apples, cored*	*½ cup grapefruit juice*

Juice together the strawberries, apples and carrot. Stir in the grapefruit juice.

Melon Pick-Up

pulp from ½ melon (about 1 *cup)*	*½ cup skimmed milk*

Put the melon pulp and the milk in a blender and process until the melon has been liquified. It's a delicious way to get all of the Vitamin A, Vitamin C and potassium of melon with the calcium and protein of milk.

Serves One.

Instant Breakfast

1 *cup fortified milk (see be-*   1 *egg*
  low)   1 *tablespoon honey*
1 *tablespoon brewer's yeast*   2 *tablespoons carob powder*

Mix all ingredients in a blender. 497 calories, 31 grams of protein.

Fortified Milk

1 *cup low-fat milk*
3 *tablespoons non fat dry milk*

Mix in a blender. 230 calories, 18 grams of protein.

Quick Pickup Breakfast Juice

8 *fl. oz. fresh tomato juice*
1 *tablespoon brewer's yeast*

Mix well. Serves one. Each serving contains approximately:

Calories	66
Protein	6 grams
Fat	0 grams
Carbohydrate	14 grams
Vitamin A	32% *RDA
Vitamin C	53% RDA
Thiamin	133% RDA
Riboflavin	28% RDA
Niacin	27% RDA
Calcium	5% RDA
Iron	18% RDA

* recommended daily allowance

Melon Cooler Baby

1 *cup diced, seeded ripe melon*
1 *tablespoon lime or lemon juice*

1 *tablespoon honey*
2 *tablespoons plain yogurt*

Purée all ingredients in blender. Chill.
Serves one.

Gazpacho Drink

½ *cup peeled, seeded, diced cucumber*
2 *tablespoons chopped spring onion*
16 *fl. oz. tomato juice*

1 *small clove garlic, chopped*
2 *tablespoons soy protein*
2 *teaspoons cider vinegar*
1 *tablespoon oil*
¼ *teaspoon chili powder*

Purée all ingredients in blender.
Serves Two.

Cucu-Berry

½ *cucumber, peeled, seeded and chopped*
4 *large, ripe strawberries*

½ *cup apple juice*
1 *teaspoon honey*

Purée all ingredients in blender. Chill.
Serves One.

Health Nut

3 *tablespoons plain yogurt*
½ *banana, peeled and sliced*

2 *tablespoons peanut butter*
½ *cup apple juice*

Purée all ingredients in blender. Chill.
Serves One.

Tropical Passion

1 *banana, peeled and sliced*   1 *cup apple juice*
1 *cup orange juice*   4 *large, ripe strawberries*
1 *teaspoon honey*

Purée all ingredients in a blender. Chill.
   Serves Two.

Pineapple Punch

½ *cup fresh pineapple juice**   1 *stalk celery, with leaves*
1 *carrot*

Juice the carrot and celery together and mix with the
pineapple juice.

* One average pineapple, peeled and cored, yields about three cups of
juice. The amount depends on the size and ripeness of the fruit.

Sauerkraut Cooler

1 *lb. sauerkraut (not tinned, if* 2 *medium size ripe apples,*
   possible)   *cored*
                                    1 *carrot*

Rinse the sauerkraut very well and drain it. Juice the
'kraut, apples and carrot together.

Sugar, Sweets

Ordinary table sugar, sucrose, fulfills no physiological, nutritional need, yet the average yearly intake in the United States is 102 pounds for each man, woman and child! That's roughly *one third of a pound of sugar every day!* It is as high, if not higher in this country. Sugar is found in baked goods, fruit drinks, carbonated drinks, tinned goods, convenience foods and many other items. As Dr. John Yudkin points out in his book *Sweet and Dangerous*, (Peter H. Wyden, New York, 1972) we don't associate any particular texture with sweetness.

The blood sugar which is our bodies' fuel is glucose. Glucose is synthesized from various foods as they are processed in the digestive system. In other words, we can get all the "sugar" we need without sucrose. Sucrose can be used by the body to provide energy but other foods will not only provide energy, but other nutrients as well.

The accompanying chart is based on data in McCance & Widdowson's *The Composition of Foods*, published by Her Majesty's Stationery Office. The figures are for 100 grams of food.

100 grams	Cal- cium mg.	Phos- phorus mg.	Iron mg.	Potas- sium mg.	Magne- sium mg.	Thia- min mg.	Ribo- flavin mg.	Niacin mg.	Vitamin C mg.
Sugar:									
White	2	Trace	Trace	2	Trace	0	0	0	0
Brown	53	20	0.9	89	0.15	Trace	Trace	Trace	0
Honey (Extracted)	5	6	.5	51	3	Trace	.05	.2	Trace
Black Treacle	290	69	37	1,063	81	Trace	Trace	Trace	0
Dried Dates (without stones)	59	63	3.0	684	58	.07	.04	0	0

... and Honey

From the chart, it is clear that sugar is an inferior sweetener but honey would *seem* to be undesirable as well. Actually, honey is about 17 per cent water, which lowers the percentage of nutrients when compared to the same amount of dry material. Second, honey is super-sweet and one tends to use less of it than sugar. Honey is invert or pre-digested sugar and is absorbed directly into the bloodstream. According to the American Honey Institute the average chemical composition of honey is:

Water	17.7 per cent
Levulose	40.5 per cent
Dextrose	34.0 per cent
Sucrose	1.9 per cent
Dextrins and gums	1.5 per cent
Ash*	18 per cent
Undetermined	4.2 per cent

* Silicon, copper, manganese, choline, calcium, potassium, sodium, phosphorus, sulphur, aluminium, magnesium.

In *Sweet and Dangerous*, Dr. Yudkin implicates sugar in heart disease, severe indigestion, changes of eyesight, dental caries, dermatitis, gout and possibly cancer. He also says that "sugar is sugar" and that brown is no better than white. The solution is to cut our sugar intake drastically. However, we do not agree with his advocacy of saccharine and cyclamates. *If we do not buy foods with sugar, we can control the amount and type of sugar we eat.*

Black treacle is nutritionally quite valuable but it is also strong-flavoured and not suitable for all purposes. Brown or "raw" sugar is cane or beet sugar which has been partially refined or has had molasses added. Honey tends to absorb water and so keeps cakes moist but keeps biscuits from being crisp. Date sugar has a unique flavour and does not dissolve well.

The best way to use sugar of any kind is not at all. The next best is sparingly, judiciously and informedly.

Cheesecake

CRUST

¼ *lb. wheat flour*	3 *teaspoons oil*
2 *tbs. honey*	1 *egg yolk*
⅓ *cup wheat germ*	*grated rind of one lemon*

Blend all the ingredients together. Pat to cover bottom and sides of a 10″ flan tin. Bake in a preheated 350°F. oven for 5 minutes.

FILLING

4 *eggs*	1 *teaspoon lemon juice*
10 *oz. cottage cheese*	1 *teaspoon vanilla*
½ *cup honey*	2 *egg whites, beaten stiffly*

Combine the eggs, cottage cheese, honey, lemon juice and vanilla. A little at a time, whirr the mixture in a blender* to make it smooth. Fold in the egg whites.

Pour the filling into the prepared crust and bake at 350°F. 30 minutes or until lightly browned. Let cool.

Cheesecake is delicious topped with fresh berries.

*NOTE: If you do not have a blender, rub the cottage cheese through a sieve. Beat the eggs. Combine the eggs, cheese, honey, lemon juice and vanilla, beating to mix well. Fold in the egg whites.

Fruitcake

3 *eggs, lightly beaten*	1 *teaspoon cinnamon*
1 *teacup honey*	1 *teaspoon allspice*
¾ *cup vegetable oil*	6 *oz. stoned dates, chopped*

6 *oz. stoned prunes, chopped*
6 *oz. dried apricots, chopped*
12 *oz. raisins*
3 *slices dried pineapple, chop-*
  ped
5 *oz. chopped walnuts*
3 *oz. chopped, un-blanced*
  almonds
3 *tablespoons freshly grated*
  orange peel

2 *oz. soy flour*
1 *cup non-instant milk powder*
3 *oz. wheat germ*
12 *oz. whole wheat flour*
¼ *teaspoon salt*
2 *fl. oz. boiling water*
1½ *teaspoon bicarbonate of*
  soda

Line 5 small (7″) loaf tins with greaseproof paper. Heat oven to 350°F.

Combine eggs, honey and oil and beat for two minutes or until thick and creamy. Beat in cinnamon and allspice. Mix in fruits, nuts and orange peel. Add soy flour, milk powder and wheat germ one at a time, beating well after each addition. Sift flour together with salt and stir into batter. Add bicarbonate of soda to boiling water and stir into batter. Do not stir any more than necessary to blend.

Pour batter into prepared loaf tins. Bake at 350°F. for about 45 minutes or until edges of cakes shrink from sides of pan. Remove cakes, with lining still wrapped around the cake. Cool on wire racks.

Wrap cooled cakes tightly and store in airtight containers. They will keep for at least a month. If you wish, moisten the cake with a few drops of grape juice or brandy every few days, just be sure to re-wrap them tightly.

Party Cake

3 *tbs. honey*
¼ *cup safflower oil*
1 *egg, lightly beaten*
8 *oz. whole wheat flour*
1 *teaspoon bicarbonate of soda*
¼ *teaspoon kelp powder*

1 *teaspoon cinnamon*
1 *cup chunky applesauce at*
  room temperature
5 *oz. broken walnuts*
6 *oz. raisins*

Preheat oven to 325°F. Oil an 8″ cake tin.

Blend together the honey and oil. Beat in the egg, sift the flour with the bicarbonate of soda, salt and cinnamon. Add the flour mixture to the honey mixture a little at a time, beating until smooth. Stir in the applesauce, then the raisins and the walnuts. Pour into the prepared tin.

Bake at 325°F. 30 to 40 minutes or until a skewer tests clean. Slide a knife around the edges to loosen cake. Cool on a wire rack.

Applesauce Cake

¼ cup safflower oil
2 cups applesauce
6 oz. whole wheat flour
2 oz. wheat germ
½ teacup honey

1 teaspoon bicarbonate of soda
1 teaspoon cinnamon
½ teaspoon allspice
3 oz. raisins

Heat oven to 350°F.. Oil 9-inch square cake tin.

Mix all ingredients together in the order listed. Pour batter into oiled tin, spreading evenly.

Bake 30 minutes or until top springs back when touched lightly. Serve hot or cold.

This is a very moist cake which travels in lunchboxes quite well.

Cherry-Orange Cake
Good for lunchboxes

2 tbs. honey
1 cup dried cherries
1 tablespoon grated orange rind
3 tablespoons oil

2 eggs, separated
½ lb. whole wheat flour
2 teaspoons baking powder
6 fl. oz. milk

Heat the honey, cherries, and orange rind slowly to a boil. Remove from heat and let stand 30 minutes.

Heat oven to 350°F. Oil an 8″ × 8″ × 3″ baking tin.

Mix together the oil and egg yolks. Beat the whites until frothy. Mix the flour and baking powder together, stir into the oil-egg yolk mixture, then the milk. Stir in the honey and cherries. Mix well. Add half of the egg whites, mix lightly, and then fold in the remainder of the whites. Spread the mixture in the prepared tin.

Bake 25–30 minutes. Cool on a wire rack.

Makes 12–16 squares.

Holiday Cake
Our "birthday standard"

3 *tbs. honey*
¼ *cup vegetable oil*
1 *egg, beaten*
7 *oz. whole wheat flour*
1 *teaspoon bicarbonate of soda*
¼ *teaspoon salt*

1 *teaspoon cinnamon*
1 *cup applesauce, at room temperature*
5 *oz. broken walnuts*
6 *oz. raisins or chopped dates*

Preheat oven to 325°F. Oil an 8-inch cake tin.

Blend the honey with the oil. Beat in the egg. Sift the flour with the bicarbonate of soda, salt and cinnamon. Add the flour mixture to the honey mixture a little at a time, beating until smooth. Stir in the applesauce, then the raisins and walnuts. Pour into the prepared tin.

Bake at 325°F. for 30–40 minutes, or until a skewer tests clean.

Loosen the cake by sliding a knife along the edges.

Cool on a wire rack.

Custard Tarts

CRUST
4 *oz. whole wheat flour*
2 *oz. bran*
2 *teaspoons sugar (light brown)*

⅓ *cup oil*
2 *tablespoons milk*
1 *egg*

Mix all crust ingredients together and form 12 small balls. Press balls into 12 oiled patty-pans to form bottoms and sides of tart shells. Chill well.

Heat oven to 425°F.

CUSTARD

2 *tbs. honey*   1½ *oz. chopped walnuts*
2 *eggs*   1 *cup plain yogurt*
3 *oz. chopped dried apricots*   ½ *oz. toasted wheat germ.*

Mix eggs and honey together until well mixed. Stir in remaining custard ingredients. Divide custard evenly into the tart shells.

Bake in preheated oven for about 25 minutes or until a knife inserted in the centre of a custard comes out clean.
Makes 12.

Honey-Yogurt Custard

4 *eggs, lightly beaten*   1 *oz. wheat germ*
4 *tablespoons honey*   ½ *pint plain yogurt*
2 *teaspoons orange flower wa-*
    ter OR 1 teaspoon vanilla

Preheat oven to 325°F. Butter a 2 pint ovenproof dish, or 6 individual custard cups.

Add the honey, orange flower water and wheat germ to the eggs and beat well. Add the yogurt and mix thoroughly. Pour the mixture into the prepared baking dish. Place the baking dish or custard cups in a pan containing about 1 inch of very warm water. Bake for about 1 hour, or until a knife inserted into the centre of the custard comes out clean.
Serves 6.

Walnut Honey Tart

1 8-inch pie crust, unbaked
2 eggs, beaten
½ teacup honey

1 teaspoon vanilla
6 oz. shelled walnuts
pinch salt

Heat oven to 375°F.

Beat honey and eggs together. Beat in vanilla and salt. Place walnuts in pie crust. Pour egg-honey mixture over walnuts. Bake for about 30 minutes, or until set.

Rice Pudding

6 oz. brown rice
1¾ pints boiling water
1 cup non-instant powdered milk
3 tablespoons honey

1 teaspoon vanilla
2 eggs
5 oz. raisins
¼ teaspoon allspice powder
pinch salt

Pour the boiling water over the rice and let stand 1 hour. Pre-heat oven to 350°F.

Whisk the milk powder into the rice mixture. Add all other ingredients and mix well.

Pour mixture into a 2-pint casserole and bake at 350°F. for 20 minutes. Reduce heat to 325°. and continue cooking for 40 minutes more, or until the pudding is set.

Serve warm or cool — especially good with cream!
Serves 4–6.

Carob Brownies

3 oz. whole wheat flour
2 tablespoons carob powder
½ teaspoon salt
1 tablespoon brewers' yeast
½ cup non-instant dry milk powder

⅓ cup vegetable oil
½ cup honey
2 eggs
1 teaspoon vanilla
3 oz. chopped walnuts

Heat oven to 325°F. Oil and flour an 8″ square tin.

Sift together flour, carob, salt, yeast and milk powder. mix vegetable oil with honey. Beat in eggs, one at a time. Stir in vanilla. Beat in dry ingredients. Fold in nuts. Pour batter into prepared tin.

Bake at 325°F. for 25 minutes or until skewer comes out clean. Cut in squares while still warm. Leave in the tin until cool.

Makes about 2 dozen.

Pineapple Coconut Bars
(Very sweet)

4 oz. whole wheat flour	5 tbs. honey
⅓ cup vegetable oil	

TOPPING

2 eggs	1 teaspoon baking powder
5 tbs. honey	2 slices sun-dried pineapple,
1 teaspoon vanilla	chopped
2 oz. whole wheat flour	3 oz. shredded coconut
1 tablespoon brewers' yeast	3 oz. broken walnuts

Oil an 8″ square baking tin. Heat oven to 350°F.

Mix together 4 oz. of whole wheat flour, vegetable oil and honey. Pat mixture with your fingers to spread it on the bottom of the pan. Bake at 350°F. for 10 minutes.

Meanwhile, mix topping. Mix together eggs, honey and vanilla. Mix 2 oz. whole wheat flour with yeast and baking powder. Stir egg mixture into flour mixture until smooth. Stir in the pineapple, coconut and walnuts. Spread topping mixture over still-warm crust and bake 15 minutes more.

Cool on wire rack. Cut into bars or squares and sprinkle with non-instant powdered milk.

Tiger Bars

5 *tablespoons vegetable oil*
3 *tablespoons honey*
1 *tablespoon liquid lecithin*
½ *cup dark molasses or black*
   treacle
2 *eggs, lightly beaten*
6 *oz. whole wheat flour*
2 *oz. soy flour*

⅓ *cup non-instant dry milk*
1½ *teaspoon baking powder*
1 *teaspoon ground cinnamon*
¼ *teaspoon ground cloves*
¼ *teaspoon powdered ginger*
6 *oz. raisins*
3 *oz. chopped nuts OR seeds*
   OR soy granules

Heat oven to 350°F. Oil and flour an 8″ × 13″ baking tin. Mix together the oil, honey, lecithin, molasses and eggs. Mix the dry ingredients together. Add the oil mixture to the dry ingredients, mixing well. Stir in the raisins and nuts. Place the mixture in the baking tin and bake for 10–15 minutes, or until done. Cut in 1 inch squares. Let cool in the pan.

Oatmeal Drops

3 *oz. whole wheat flour*
½ *teaspoon salt*
½ *teaspoon bicarbonate of soda*
2 *fl. oz. oil*
3 *oz. date sugar (or unrefined*
   white sugar)

2 *tbs. honey*
2 *eggs*
1 *teaspoon vanilla*
6 *oz. rolled oats*
3 *oz. chopped walnuts*

Heat oven to 300°F.

Mix flour with salt and bicarbonate of soda. Add the oil, sugar, honey, eggs and vanilla. Stir until smooth. Fold in oatmeal and nuts.

Drop batter by teaspoonfuls onto ungreased baking sheets. These biscuits do not spread much. Bake at 300°F. for 7 to 12 minutes, depending on size of biscuits. Watch them, as they do brown quickly. Cool on wire racks.

Makes about 5 dozen.

Fruit Snacks
Great for lunch bags and hungry kids

3 *tablespoons sesame seeds*
6 *oz. seedless raisins*
6 *oz. unsulphured, sun-dried*
  apricots

1 *tablespoon wheat germ*
4 *tablespoons sunflower seeds*
2 *tablespoons soy granules*
2 *tablespoons grated coconut*

Toast the sesame seeds in a heavy frying pan until they begin to "jump." Remove from the pan.

Chop the raisins and apricots together. Add the sesame seeds, wheat germ, sunflower seeds and soy granules. Add one tablespoon of the grated coconut. Mix as well as you can and squeeze the mixture into one-inch balls. If it is too sticky, add the remaining one tablespoon of coconut. (The stickiness depends on how moist the apricots are.) Keep in a covered jar in the refrigerator.

Honey Peanut Candy

1¼ *cups non-instant powdered*
   milk
1 *cup unsalted peanut butter*
1 *cup honey*

1 *teaspoon lemon juice*
½ *cup sunflower seeds*
shredded coconut

Mix together powdered milk, peanut butter, honey and lemon juice. Mix in sunflower seeds. Form little balls about 1″ and roll balls in coconut. Keep in refrigerator, wrapped well.

About 5 dozen 1″ balls.

Apple Soufflé

4 *egg yolks*
2 *tablespoons honey*
1 *tablespoon whole wheat flour*
6 *fl. oz. milk*

pinch cinnamon
2 *apples, peeled, cored and*
  sliced
2 *teaspoons oil*

1 *teaspoon honey*   ½ *teaspoon cream of tartar*
5 *egg whites*   ½ *teaspoon salt*

Oil a large soufflé dish. If it is a shallow soufflé dish, add a
collar of oiled, waxed paper. We prefer a charlotte mould,
which does not require a collar.

Heat oven to 400°F.

Beat the egg yolks with the 2 tablespoons honey and
flour. Cook, stirring, over low heat, adding the milk
slowly. Add the cinnamon, and stir over low heat to make
a sauce the consistency of thick cream. Remove from heat.

Heat the apple slices with the oil and 1 teaspoon of
honey, cover the pot and let simmer about 5 minutes, or
until the slices are soft. Remove from heat.

Beat the egg whites with the cream of tartar and salt to
form stiff peaks. Add about ⅓ of the egg whites to the egg
yolk mixture, mix gently. Fold in the remaining whites.
Pour half of the egg mixture into the soufflé dish, add a
layer of apples, reserving 1 or 2 slices for garnish. Add the
rest of the egg mixture, top with the reserved apple slices.
Bake for 15 to 20 minutes.

Serves 6.

Soy-Apple Betty

oil   1 *tablespoon lemon juice*
2 *oz. soy granules*   4 *medium apples, cored and*
2 *oz. wheat germ*   *sliced thin*
¼ *teacup honey*   *cinnamon*
½ *cup warm water*

Heat oven to 350°F. Oil a 8″ × 8″ baking tin.

Mix the granules, wheat germ, honey, water and lemon
juice. Place half of the sliced apples in a layer on the
bottom of the baking dish, top with half of the granule
mixture. Sprinkle with cinnamon to taste. Add a layer of
the remaining apples, top with the remaining granule
mixture, sprinkle with cinnamon and cover the tin tightly
with tin foil.

Bake covered for 30 minutes. Remove the foil and bake 5 to 10 minutes more or until the topping is crisp.
Serves 4–6.

Yogurt Iced Lollies

2 cups plain yogurt
¼ cup undiluted fruit juice con-
* centrate, any flavour*

Mix the yogurt and fruit concentrate thoroughly and pour into paper cups. Freeze until slushy, then stand a wooden stick in each cup for a handle and freeze until firm. To serve, just peel away the paper cup.

Dried Fruit Compote

12 oz. mixed dried fruits (any
* combination you like)*
3 oz. raisins
1 orange, seeded and sliced thin
1 cup water

3 tbs. honey
2 sticks cinnamon
2 cloves
2 slices fresh ginger (if avail-
* able)*

Mix fruits and raisins together in slow-cooker — arrange the orange on top of the fruit. Bring the water to a boil in a small pan and add the honey. Pour the hot mixture over the fruits. Tuck in the cinnamon sticks, cloves and ginger. Cover and cook at LOW for 4 to 6 hours.
Serves 6.

Strawberry Ice

8 fl. oz. water
3 tablespoons flaked agar-
* agar*

½ lb. strawberries, hulled and
* sliced*
½ teacup honey
8 fl. oz. orange juice

Heat water to boiling, add agar-agar and simmer for about 4 minutes. Set aside.

Purée strawberries with honey in the blender. Add half of the orange juice. Add the remaining orange juice to the agar-agar and mix well. Add mixture to blender. Blend thoroughly.

Freeze the mixture in ice trays, stirring every half hour or so.

Makes 6 servings.

Weights and Measures

28 grams = 1 ounce
100 grams = 3½ ounces
454 grams = 1 pound
1 teaspoon = 5 mililitres
1½ pints = approximately 1 litre

1000 micrograms = 1 milligram
1000 milligrams = 1 gram
·001 grams = 1 milligram
·001 milligrams = 1 microgram

100°F = 38°C warm water
180°F = 82°C very hot water
250°F = 121°C very slow oven
300°F = 149°C slow oven
325°F = 163°C slow oven
350°F = 177°C moderate oven
375°F = 191°C moderate oven
400°F = 204°C hot oven
425°F = 218°C hot oven
450°F = 232°C very hot oven

To convert °F to °C, subtract
32°, multiply by 5, and divide
by 9 [(°F−32) × 5 ÷ 9 = °C].

Index

NOTE: Recipes with * are meatless main dishes

NOTE: Recipes with * are meatless main dishes

NOTE: Recipes with * are meatless main dishes

NOTE: Recipes with * are meatless main dishes

NOTE: Recipes with * are meatless main dishes

224   *The Healthy Gourmet Cookbook*

NOTE: Recipes with * are meatless main dishes

NOTE: Recipes with * are meatless main dishes

NOTE: Recipes with * are meatless main dishes

NOTE: Recipes with * are meatless main dishes